D1603973

THE CULTS OF OSTIA

Navis oneraria.

From a relief in the Museo Torlonia.

The ship is supposed to be in the harbour of the Tiber at Ostia, the statues on pedestals and the flaming altar at the top of the scene being on the quay. The mast is surmounted by a Victory carrying a wreath and palm. The mainsail is decorated with the wolf and twins. Another figure of Victory is on the stern, which also has a goose-head (χηνίσκος). In the after-part of the vessel is a cabin with two windows. In the fore-part one of the crew is dressing a piece of wood with an adze, while another is hauling at a rope which runs through a block at the end of the foremast and thence to the mooring-post on the quay. The halyard which runs to the bow works through a block (fastened to the mast, but hidden by the staysails) and supports the yard-arm (*antenna*). The shrouds (*funes antarii*) of the mast, the brails and sheets of the sail, and the brace attached to the left end of the yard-arm are well shown.

THE CULTS OF OSTIA

GREEK & ROMAN GODS—
IMPERIAL CULT-ORIENTAL GODS

BY

LILY ROSS TAYLOR

ARES PUBLISHERS INC.
CHICAGO   MCMLXXVI

Unchanged Reprint of the Edition:
Baltimore, 1913
ARES PUBLISHERS INC.
612 N. Michigan Avenue
Chicago, Illinois 60611
Printed in the United States of America
International Standard Book Number:
0-89005-114-3

CONTENTS

LIST OF ABBREVIATIONS

Ann. dell'Inst.—*Annali dell'Instituto di corrispondenza archeologica.*

Bull. dell'Inst.—*Bulletino dell'Instituto di corrispondenza archeologica.*

CIG.—*Corpus Inscriptionum Graecarum.*

CIL.[1]—*Corpus Inscriptionum Latinarum.*

EE.—*Ephemeris Epigraphica.*

IG.—*Inscriptiones Graecae.*

Mél.—*Mélanges d'Archéologie et d'Histoire del'École française de Rome.*

NS.—*Notizie degli Scavi di Antichità.*

Pauly-Wissowa—Pauly-Wissowa, *Real Encyclopaedie der classischen Altertumswissenschaft.*

Roscher—Roscher, *Ausführliches Lexicon der griechischen und römischen Mythologie.*

Ruggiero—Ruggiero, *Dizionario epigrafico di Antichità romane.*

---

[1] Inscriptions cited by number only are from Vol. XIV. The inscriptions have been quoted without the indication of the divisions of the lines, and, in general, without the use of *sic* to show unusual or ungrammatical forms.

INTRODUCTION

Ostia, the port of Rome, was situated at the mouth of the Tiber about sixteen miles from the metropolis. Under the name Ostia I include not only the original settlement on the south bank of the Tiber, but also the city, known as Portus, which grew up about the harbors of Claudius and Trajan two miles north of the river's mouth. Ostia was a city of considerable size during the second and third centuries after Christ. In the extent of its ruins and in the number of its inscriptions it is surpassed only by Rome and Pompeii in Italy. And yet its history and topography have received a relatively small share of attention. This neglect is due, at least in part, to the desultory and unscientific character of most of the excavations, and to the fact that, even when the excavations have been carefully conducted, the results have often been inadequately published.[1] At present, however, great interest is being aroused in this site by the more thorough work that is now in process there. Systematic excavations, begun in 1907 under the direction of the Italian Ministry of Public Instruction, bid fair to continue for

[1] The earliest excavations at Ostia, those of the Scotchman Gavin Hamilton and of the Englishman Robert Fagan at the end of the eighteenth century, were conducted simply in search of works of art and were never published. Excavations were carried on under various auspices intermittently throughout the nineteenth century, and accounts and discussions of them occurred in various journals, such as the *Annali* and *Bulletino dell'Instituto di correspondenza archeologica.* Since 1876 accounts of the work have appeared in the *Notizie degli Scavi di Antichità.* See Paschetto, *Ostia, colonia romana,* pp. 485 ff.

1

some years.[2]   Very valuable results have already been obtained, and more may be expected in the future.   A great
service has been rendered archæologists by the prompt publication of the finds by Professor Dante Vaglieri who is in
charge of the work at Ostia.   In addition to this, Signore
L. Paschetto has recently published a comprehensive monograph dealing with the history and topography of the city.[3]
Important contributions to these subjects have also been
made by M. Carcopino [4] of the French school in Rome.[5]

These recent discoveries and researches have provided
new and valuable evidence for the history of the city, which
is still, however, obscure in many important details.   Before
proceeding to a discussion of the various cults of Ostia, it
is desirable to outline briefly those facts in the history of
the city which are essential to the understanding of such a
study.

According to a tradition never questioned by Roman
historians, Ostia, which was generally supposed to be the
first colony of Rome, was founded by King Ancus Marcius.[6]
Ennius (*Ann.* ii. frg. 22 V [2]) and Polybius (vi. 2, 9), whose

---

[2] *Vide NS.* 1907 ff.

[3] *Ostia, colonia romana, storia e monumenti.*   Prefazione di Dante
Vaglieri, in *Dissertazioni della pont. accad. rom. di arch.*   Ser. ii, Tomo
x, 1912, pp. 1-593.   3 plans.

[4] On the port of Claudius, *NS.* 1907, pp. 734-740; on the mosaic of
the barracks of the *vigiles*, *Mél.* 1907, pp. 227-241.   A series of articles
entitled *Ostiensia* by Carcopino is now appearing in the *Mélanges
d'Archéologie et d'Histoire de l'École française de Rome.*   Thus far
four have appeared:—I. *Glanures épigraphiques*, 1909, pp. 341-364;
II. *Le Quartier des docks*, 1910, pp. 397-446; III. *Les inscriptions
gamaliennes*, 1911, pp. 143-230; IV. *Notes complémentaires*, 1911, pp.
365-368.   Cf. also *Les récentes fouilles d'Ostie, Journal des Savants,*
1911, pp. 448-468.

[5] It is fortunate that the inscriptions have been published by so
careful a scholar as Dessau.   See *CIL.* xiv (1887), nos. 1-2085; 4127-
4175; *EE.* vii (1892), nos. 1190-1233; *ibid.* ix (1910), nos. 433-570.
Another supplement containing inscriptions of Ostia is soon to appear.

[6] Livy i. 33; xxvii. 38; Dionys. iii. 44; Cic. *De Rep.* ii. 18, 23.

common source was probably Fabius Pictor, preserve the tradition of the early date, without mentioning a colony there. Fabius may have drawn upon a legend current in his day, or perhaps he found his information in the pontifical records. But since the data for the regal period in these records had been composed entirely of legendary matter,[7] we must conclude that the story of the founding of Ostia is no more worthy of credence than the rest of the history of the kings, as reported by Fabius. The sum of our knowledge is that before the end of the third century B. C. a legend was current to the effect that the city of Ostia was founded several centuries before, though not certainly as a colony. In Cicero's day tradition held that Ancus Marcius had also established the colony, and Festus is the only writer who indicates that it was not established until after the foundation of the city by Ancus. Compare Festus, p. 197 M. *Ostiam urbem ad exitum Tiberis in mare fluentis Ancus Marcius rex condidisse et feminino appellasse vocabulo fertur; quod sive ad urbem sive ad coloniam quae postea condita est refertur.*

This tradition of the early foundation of the colony at Ostia has not been questioned until recently. Vaglieri has noted [8] that so far the excavations in the tombs on the present site have brought to light no objects which can be dated before the third century, and that there are no references to the existence of a naval station at Ostia [9] before the

---

[7] Enmann, *Rheinisches Museum*, 1902, pp. 517 ff.; Cichorius s. v. *Annales Maximi*, Pauly-Wissowa.

[8] *NS.* 1910, p. 550 n. 1; *Bull. Com.* 1911, pp. 244 f. Introduction to Paschetto, *op. cit.* pp. xxiv f. Cf. also Carcopino, *Journal des Savants*, 1911, p. 467.

[9] Vaglieri notes that the city must have been established before the institution of the *quaestores classici* in 267 B. C. Cf. Mommsen, *Römisches Staatsrecht*, ii. p. 570; Herzog, *Römische Staatsverfassung*, i. pp. 823-825, shows that there is no good reason for calling the quaestor stationed at Ostia a *quaestor classicus.*

time of the Hannibalic War.[10]   In attempting to date the
colony, some aid may be obtained from considerations of an
economic nature.

The tract of land that belonged to Ostia was confined by
the Tiber and the Laurentian territory to a very few square
miles of marshy or sandy land which was quite unfit for
cultivation.   It could not, therefore, have served the purposes of an agricultural colony.   There are, however, two
reasons why the site might have been desirable to the Romans
at an early period—first, the ease with which salt could be
procured at this point, and second, the value of the locality
for a port.   Let us consider whether either of these reasons
might have led Rome to plant a colony here early in her
history.

Salt works were said to have been established by Ancus
Marcius at the time of the foundation of Ostia.[11]   Since
Rome must have procured her salt from the region about
the mouth of the Tiber [12] from the earliest times, it is
probable that Rome's object in seizing the region was to
gain control of the *Salinae*.   It is very likely that a village
inhabited by laborers in the *Salinae* sprang up here very
early.   The salt industry, however, though not privately
owned, was controlled in early times by contract and not
directly by the state.[13]   Furthermore Rome was very slow
to adopt a policy of furnishing state protection even to
quasi-public business interests.   The existence of salt-works
in the region cannot therefore explain the establishment of
a colony of Roman citizens at Ostia.

[10] Further evidence is supplied by a number of republican coins discovered in 1909.   No coins were found which could be dated before
254 B. C.   Cf. Carcopino, *l. c.* p. 467.

[11] Livy I. 33; Pliny, *H. N.* XXXI. 41, 89.

[12] The salt works on the north bank of the river seem to have been
older.   Cf. Nissen, *Italische Landeskunde*, II. p. 543, 566.

[13] Cf. Marquardt, *Römische Staatsverwaltung*, II. pp. 159 ff.; Ros-
towzew, *Philol.* Supp. IX. p. 411.

The need of a port for Rome's growing commerce is the reason generally assigned by both ancient and modern authorities for the early establishment of a colony at Ostia.[14] And yet the indications are that until the third century B. C. Rome had little interest in commerce.[15] There is slight evidence that the Greeks had met Roman traders before that time. Moreover, before 282 Rome had been bound by a treaty with Tarentum which prevented her ships from passing the Lacinian headlands—a treaty which could not have been signed by any state that had the least real interest in maritime commerce.[16] Further indications of the same fact may be found in Rome's failure to build a navy before the First Punic War, in the relatively small amount of foreign ware dating from the early Republic as yet discovered in Roman excavations, and, finally, in the insignificance of the coinage issued from the Roman mint before the year 268 B. C. In view of the facts, therefore, that very few Romans engaged in maritime commerce before the third century and that the state was always unwilling to incur public expense even for domestic, not to speak of foreign enterprises, it is difficult to believe that Rome for commercial reasons could have founded a colony of citizens at the Tiber's mouth long before the third century.

The original settlement in the neighborhood of Ostia, then, was probably made up chiefly of people connected with the *Salinae*.[17] Since the results of excavations indicate that the settlement on the present site is not of great antiquity, the suggestion that the original village may have been nearer to Rome than was the later city commends itself.[18] Perhaps

[14] Dionys. III. 44; Isidorus, *Orig.* xv. 1. 56; Jung, *Geographie von Italien*, p. 31; Nissen, *Italische Landeskunde*, II. pp. 566-567.

[15] On Rome's commerce cf. Blümner, *Privatleben der Römer*, pp. 618 ff.

[16] Polybius, III. 22.

[17] This is the opinion of Vaglieri, *l. c.*

[18] This suggestion was made first by Canina, *Dissertazioni dell'accad. pontif. di Archeologia*, VII (1838), pp. 265 ff. Cf. Dessau *CIL.* XIV

Festus, in the passage quoted above, preserved the truth
with regard to the subsequent foundation of the colony, even
if he is too credulous in adopting the legend about Ancus
Marcius.

Although it is impossible to determine when the colony
was established here, general considerations enable us to fix
upon a probable date. The recent excavations have made
it seem likely that the present site was not inhabited before
the third century B. C. The bold appearance of Roman ships
at Tarentum in 282, in violation of the terms of the treaty,
indicates that Roman shipping was assuming important pro-
portions in the early third century. So far as we know,
the earliest maritime colonies were planted at Antium (338
B. C.) and at Tarracina (329), sea-coast towns which had
fallen to Rome in the Latin War.[19] The fact that in 317
the Antiates complained to the Senate *se sine legibus certis,
sine magistratibus agere* (Livy IX. 20) shows that Rome,
still inexperienced in the management of colonies of citizens,
had not yet evolved her later system under which *duumviri*
and *aediles* were the regular magistrates of these colonies.[20]

p. 3, n. 8. Recently it has received support from Vaglieri, *l. c.* But
the theory of Canina that the city was gradually extended along the
river as the coast line advanced has not been supported by the results
of the excavations. The present site seems to have been laid out at
the time of its occupation along lines that held throughout its
history. Cf. Carcopino, *Journal des Savants*, 1911, pp. 466 f.

[19] Cf. Kornemann, s. v. *coloniae*, Pauly-Wissowa, cols. 520 ff.

[20] Beloch, *Der italische Bund*, 1880, p. 114, makes the statement:
"Die Verfassung der See-colonien war im Allgemeinen der der Colonien
lateinischen Rechts nachgebildet. Wie dort, so stehen auch hier 2
Praetoren an der Spitze der Stadt, die sich z. B. in Castrum Novum
bis in die Kaiserzeit hinein erhalten haben. Die *Praetores sacris Vol-
cano* (*sic*) *faciundis*, die wir später in Ostia finden, scheinen zu be-
weisen, dass einst auch dieser Stadt Praetoren vorstanden, wenn auch
in Folge der augusteischen Colonisation hier die Duumviralverfassung
eingeführt worden ist. Dagegen in den nach dem hannibalischen
Kriege deducirten Seecolonien haben sich die obersten Magistrate nicht
mehr Praetoren genannt, sondern Duumviri." Beloch's conclusion is

In 296 Rome continued her policy of securing the sea-coast for herself by planting colonies of citizens at Minturnae and Sinuessa. Probably earlier than this, but not much earlier than 300 B. C., she saw the desirability of safeguarding her commerce and her natural harbor by placing a colony of citizens at the mouth of the Tiber, a locality that had long been her undisputed possession.

At the time of the Second Punic War Ostia was already a walled town and a very important naval station.[21] When in 207 citizens of a number of maritime colonies petitioned for exemption from military service, the request was granted only to Ostia and Antium (Livy xxvii. 38). Citizens of these two places were, however, required not to be absent from their towns more than thirty days at a time when a foreign foe was in Italy. But when these two cities with several others requested exemption from service in the fleet in 191, the petition was not granted (Livy xxxvi. 3).

During the period of the Republic, Ostia had no harbor, and so ships were forced to land in the mouth of the Tiber.[22]

not supported by the facts. We shall consider later the question of the praetors of Vulcan of Ostia. The case of Castrum Novum in Picenum, which is known to have had praetors, is of very doubtful value as evidence, since it is by no means certain whether the colony of citizens of the third century was established there or at the city of the same name in Etruria. Of the citizen-colonies supposed to have been founded before the time of the Gracchi, the only one which is known to have had praetors is Auximum, and the evidence for the establishment of a colony there (Velleius I. 15, 3) is by no means certain. There seems no reason to believe that the citizen-colonies were ever governed as the Latin colonies were. They were probably governed by *duumviri* from the first. Moreover, there is no support for Beloch's supposition that Augustus reorganized Ostia or that he altered the administrative system of the colony.

[21] Carcopino (*Mél.* 1911, p. 155, n. 2) calls attention to the reference to the wall of Ostia in Livy xxvii. 23, 3. For other references to Ostia as a naval station cf. Livy xxii. 11 and 37; xxiii. 38; xxv. 20; xxvii. 22.

[22] Dionys. iii. 44; Polyb. xxxi. 20, 11.

Indeed the alluvial deposit made by the river, which has now built the land out three miles beyond ancient Ostia, had, as early as the latter part of the Republic, made it impossible for larger ships to cross the bar at the mouth of the river and reach the channel. Strabo (v. 3, 5, p. 231) described in very strong terms the disadvantages and dangers of the port in his day (*ca.* 20 B. C.), and thought it surprising that ships still came there. Caesar planned to remedy matters by constructing an artificial harbor, but his death prevented the fulfilment of the plan (Plutarch, *Caes.* 58).

Long before the time of Caesar, Rome had secured as a second port Puteoli, which, though about a hundred and fifty miles distant, commended itself because of its excellent harbor. Puteoli had first been necessary to Rome for military purposes during the Punic Wars. But it was undoubtedly her growing commerce that caused her to establish a custom house there in 199 and five years later a colony of Roman citizens. Since Southern Italy was already in far closer contact with the Orient than Rome was, it is not surprising that Puteoli became Rome's emporium for trade with the Orient and especially with Egypt.[23]

Ostia remained, throughout the Republic and early Empire, the chief port for the grain supply, and seems also to have been in closer relationship with the Occident than was Puteoli.[24] But the superiority of Puteoli's facilities as a port is at least partially responsible for the fact that so few monuments and inscriptions of the Republic and early Empire have been found at Ostia. Though the excavations now in progress are bringing to light important remains of republican buildings, so far there is very little evidence for the history of the colony during that period and the early

[23] Cf. Charles Dubois, *Pouzzoles antique, Bibliothèque des Écoles françaises d'Athènes et de Rome*, Vol. 98, Paris, 1907, pp. 65 ff. For a comparison of Ostia and Puteoli *vide* pp. 78 ff.

[24] Dubois, *op. cit.* p. 79, is probably right in drawing this inference from Pliny, *H. N.* XIX. 3.

Empire. The city seems not to have become important before the time of Claudius.

Caesar's plan of making a good harbor was finally carried out by Claudius, who did not attempt to make the port at Ostia; he chose a site two miles to the north, which he connected with the Tiber by means of a canal. Here he built an artificial basin and constructed a lighthouse. The work had already been begun in 42 A. D.[25] Representations of the port on coins of Nero indicate that it was not finally dedicated until the reign of that emperor [26] to whose jealousy is due the fact that it was called Portus Augusti rather than Portus Claudii. Even this harbor proved inadequate to the needs of the shipping, and accordingly it was enlarged by Trajan. An hexagonal basin was constructed inside the port of Claudius and was given the name Portus Traiani. Considerable remains of both basins may be seen today. A flourishing town with many important public buildings soon sprang up about the port, from which it received the name Portus.[27]

Although Portus was two miles distant from the old town of Ostia and separated from it by the Tiber, until the fourth century the two cities were under the same municipal organization and had the same magistrates and priests.[28] Ostia proper, far from decreasing in importance after the new port was built, became a large commercial city, with perhaps 50,000 inhabitants.[29] The remains of the city, which date

[25] Cassius Dio, LX. 11. Cf. *CIL.* XIV 85.

[26] Cohen, *Médailles impériales*, I. Nero, 33-41.

[27] The best discussion of the remains of Portus is that of Lanciani, *Ann. dell'Inst.* 1868, pp. 144 ff. Lanciani's plan of the harbor of Trajan is given in *Mon. dell'Inst.* VIII. Pl. XLIX. The excavations at Portus, which have not been continued since 1870, have been incomplete and unscientific. The most fruitful work has been that on the Torlonia estate. On the port of Claudius cf. Carcopino, *NS.* 1907, pp. 734 ff.

[28] Cf. Dessau, *op. cit.* p. 6.

[29] See Paschetto, *op. cit.* p. 187.

chiefly from the second and third centuries after Christ, seem to show that it was almost entirely rebuilt after the construction of the port. Inscriptions furnish much valuable evidence for the history of the colony during this period. The emperors of the second century seem to have been particularly zealous in adorning the city.

The population of Ostia during this period was largely of the middle and lower classes. Aristocratic Romans, although they owned villas along the neighboring coast, seem not to have been attracted to Ostia. The commercial character of the population is well shown by the large number of professional *collegia* attested in the inscriptions. Traders from the East who had hitherto flocked to Puteoli began to come to Ostia after the construction of the port of Claudius. When later Trajan's port afforded still greater facilities for landing near Rome, the Campanian city declined markedly in importance, as her northern rival rose.[30]

Most of our evidence for the religious history of Ostia falls within the two centuries following the establishment of the new port. This was the period when Oriental religions were everywhere undermining the old Roman beliefs and religious forms. At Ostia, where there was more constant contact with the East than elsewhere, the old cults had a particularly difficult and often an unsuccessful struggle to hold their own. The most important Oriental worships were firmly established here in the second century. Christianity early gained a strong foothold, and the later history of Ostia and Portus is closely bound up with the history of the Church.[31]

[30] Cf. Dubois, *op. cit.* p. 81. In 172 A. D. the Tyrians of Puteoli complained of the decrease in numbers and wealth of their colony.

[31] The later history of Ostia and Portus is in many details obscure. See Vaglieri's interesting comments (*NS.* 1910, p. 106) on a recently discovered inscription of Ragonius Vincentius Celsus *vir clarissimus,* who seems to have erected a statue to *Urbs* which was paid for by the inhabitants of Ostia.

The present study is, however, concerned only with the pagan cults of Ostia. The evidence for these cults is, of course, mainly epigraphical, and, as we have indicated, dates chiefly from the second and third centuries after Christ. Inscriptions of religious significance, while they are rare in the first century of the Empire, are, with one possible exception, entirely lacking for the Republic.[32] In that period our only direct evidence for the religion of the city is found in one of the rare literary references which give information about the cults of Ostia (Livy xxxii. 1, 10). Finds of statues and reliefs supplement our knowledge of the cults of the city.[33] Especially important is the bas-relief found at Portus, now in the Museo Torlonia, which gives a view of the harbor of Claudius.[34]

The most important evidence for the history of the Church at Ostia is summarized by Dessau, *CIL.* xiv p. 5. See Paschetto, *op. cit.* pp. 177 ff. Evidence for the presence of Jews has been found at Portus. Cf. *ibid.* pp. 175 ff.

[32] While further excavations will doubtless add to the list of shrines, it is hardly probable that new cults of importance will be discovered. The list of the priests of the colony must be practically complete.

[33] It is doubtful how far one may venture to use the statues, reliefs, etc. found at Ostia and Portus as evidence for the cults of these cities. Statues of Venus and Bacchus, for instance, were used so much by the Romans for ornamental purposes, that it is doubtful whether one may attach any religious significance to such statues discovered at Ostia. If the interesting winged female statue recently discovered at Ostia represents Athena Victrix, as Savignoni believes it does (*Ausonia*, 1910, pp. 69 ff.), it cannot be regarded as evidence for the cult of that goddess in the port. The case is different with representations of Oriental gods. Many of the statues found in the excavations of the eighteenth century are in private collections in England (cf. Michaelis, *Ancient Marbles in Great Britain*, index s. v. Ostia); others are in the Vatican. Since 1800 the finds, except for a few which have been placed in the small museum at Ostia, have gone to museums in Rome, the Vatican, the Lateran, and, more recently, the National Museum. Objects found at Portus have gone chiefly to the Lateran and the Museo Torlonia. I have not attempted in this study to make a complete list of statues of the gods found in Ostia and Portus.

[34] Cf. Guglielmotti, *Delle due navi romane scolpite sul bassorilievo del*

Remains of no less than eleven temples and of several small shrines have been discovered at Ostia and Portus.[35] Only the shrines of Mithras, the form of which is unmistakable, a shrine of the emperors, and the temple of Magna Mater at Ostia can be identified beyond a doubt. Various suggestions for the identification of the other temples have been made. Sometimes, as in the case of the so-called temple of Portunus at Portus,[36] the identification has been

Museo Torlonia, Atti della pont. Accad. di Archeologia, Serie II. vol. 1, pp. 1-81; Cavedoni, *Bull. dell'Inst.* 1864, pp. 219 ff.; Henzen, *Ann. dell'Inst.* 1864, pp. 12 ff.; C. L. Visconti, *Catalogo del Museo Torlonia,* no. 430; Inscription 2033.

[35] The most important temple of Ostia is the large one on a high *podium* which was long the chief landmark of the city. It has been variously attributed to Vulcan, Jupiter Optimus Maximus, and Castor and Pollux. A temple in the centre of the so-called Forum has been identified as that of Ceres or of Roma and Augustus. Four small temples near the theatre are perhaps to be identified as those of Venus, Fortuna, Ceres, and Spes.

At Portus the only ruins of temples which may be seen today are those of the large round temple to the east of the port of Trajan, which was identified as that of Portunus on the basis of a forged inscription. Within the estate of the Torlonia family another round temple, supposed to be that of Bacchus, was found. Altmann, *Die Rundbauten in Latium,* p. 69, says of these temples: "Heute zeigt keine Spur mehr, wo beide gelegen haben." Then he gives a summary of Nibby's description of the so-called temple of Portunus, which fits excellently the temple now standing. Another small temple, of which some architectural fragments may be seen today, was unearthed to the south of the port of Trajan. This has not been identified. Within the so-called Palazzo Imperiale were found remains of still another temple which was believed to be that of Hercules.

[36] Ligorio forged several inscriptions to Portunus which he claimed to have found in the round temple at Portus discussed above. Cf. *CIL.* XIV *16, *17, *18. Portunus, who was the god of harbors, might naturally have been expected to have a temple in Ostia or Portus, and the words of Varro, *L. L.* VI. 19, have been thought to prove the existence of such a temple: *Portunalia dicta a Portuno cui eo die aedes in Portu Tiberino facta et feriae institutae.* If the words of Varro are to be referred to Rome's harbor, we must look for the temple in Ostia since there was no settlement at Portus until after the time of Varro. It is very likely, however, that Varro refers to a temple in Rome

based on spurious inscriptions, but in other cases, as for instance that of the supposed temple of Jupiter at Ostia, the evidence for the identification is very good. No attempt to solve the problems connected with these temples has been made in the present investigation for which independent topographical study has been impossible.

itself—and probably to the small circular one in the Forum Boarium which is now known as Santa Maria del Sole. Cf. Huelsen, *Dissertazioni della pont. Accad. romana di Archeologia*, Series II. 1897, pp. 262 ff.

CHAPTER I

Greek and Roman Gods

The evidence for the cults of Ostia is so late that it is useless to try to distinguish between Greek and Roman gods. The various cults have therefore been taken up so far as possible in order of the probable date of their establishment and, when this has not been possible, in order of importance.

VULCAN

Probably the oldest cult of Ostia was that of Vulcan whose temple was first in the list of those restored by P. Lucilius Gamala.[1] Compare 375, l. 21. [I]dem aedem Volcani

---

[1] Inscriptions 375 and 376 which record the benefactions of P. Lucilius Gamala to the city of Ostia have given rise to extended discussion. 375, which is not extant but rests on excellent manuscript authority, came from Portus. The *provenance* of 376, which is now in the Vatican, is not known. The latter inscription is approximately dated by the mention of a restoration by Gamala of baths constructed by .divus Pius (after 161). The differences in the benefactions recorded and in the *cursus* of Gamala as given in the two inscriptions are as baffling as are the similarities, and have led to various explanations. The most recent is that of Carcopino: *Les inscriptions gamaliennes*, *Mél.* 1911, pp. 143-230, cf. bibliography cited p. 143. Carcopino takes the view held originally by Mommsen and later by Homolle, that these inscriptions refer to two different men. The later view of Mommsen, which agrees with the opinion of Dessau, is that the two refer to the same man, who lived in the time of Hadrian, Antoninus Pius, and Marcus Aurelius. Carcopino thinks that the first Gamala (375) died in the reign of Claudius (44 B. C.) and the second (376) under Marcus Aurelius (between 166 and 180). Although Carcopino's dating of 375 in 44 B. C. is not altogether convincing, his explanation of the two inscriptions has much in its favor. In the following pages we shall refer to 375 as the inscription of the first Gamala, and to 376

sua pecunia restituit. The chief evidence for the cult is found in the titles, peculiar to Ostia, *pontifex Volcani et aedium sacrarum*,[2] *praetor* [3] and *aedilis* [4] *sacris Volcani faciundis*. These titles occur frequently in the inscriptions of Ostia, sometimes as a man's only title, and again in the *cursus* of an important member of the community.

The *pontifex Volcani et aedium sacrarum* was the chief religious officer of Ostia.[5] There seems to have been no pontifical college in the colony.[6] The title of the *pontifex* apparently indicates that at the time when the pontificate was instituted Vulcan was the most important god of Ostia. This *pontifex* was in charge of all the temples of Ostia and Portus; his permission seems to have been necessary before statues could be erected in sacred precincts or gifts of importance could be dedicated in sanctuaries. Compare 47 which records gifts made in the Sarapeum of Portus and ends

---

as that of the second Gamala. It may be well to quote here the portions of the two inscriptions which refer to the temples restored by the Gamalas: 375, ll. 21-33. [i]dem aedem Volcani sua pecunia restituit. [i]dem aedem Veneris sua pecunia constituit. [id]em aed. Fortunae sua pecunia constituit. [id]em aed. Cereris sua pecunia constituit. [id]em pondera ad macellum cum M. Turranio sua pecunia fecit. [idem] aedem Spei sua pecunia [cons]tituit. 376. ll. 13-22. idem aedem Castoris et Pollucis rest. idem curator pecuniae publicae exigendae et attribuendae in comitiis factus cellam patri Tiberino restituit. idem thermas quas divus Pius aedif[i]caverat vi ignis consumptas refecit, porticum reparavit. idem aedem Veneris impensa sua restituit.

[2] 47, 72, 132, 324, 325, 352, 4145. Differences in the abbreviations and spellings of these and the following titles are given in Dessau's lists, *CIL*. xiv p. 573.

[3] 3, 349, 390, 391, 402, 412, 415, *NS*. 1911, p. 286. For *praetor primus, secundus, tertius*, see below.

[4] 3, 351, 375, 376, 390, 391. The inscription quoted *NS*. 1910, p. 107 refers either to an aedile or to a praetor.

[5] Cf. Dessau, *CIL*. xiv p. 5.

[6] The simple title *pontifex* which occurs only in the inscriptions of the two Gamalas, in 354, and in 4128 is probably identical with the longer title.

with the words: Permissu C. Nasenni Marcelli pontificis
Volcani et aedium sacrarum et Q. Lolli Rufi Chrysidiani
et M. Aemili Vitalis Crepereiani II. vir(um). 324 records
the permission of the *pontifex* for the erection of a statue
in the *Campus Matris Deum:* [7] M. Antius Crescens Calpurnianus pontif. Volk. et aedium sacrar. statuam poni in
campo Matris Deum infantilem permisi (consular date 203
A. D.). 352 refers to the erection of a statue of a priest of
Isis, probably in sacred precincts, as is indicated by the
words: locus datus a Iulio Faustino pont. Vulk. aed. sacrar.
The importance of the office *pontifex Volcani et aedium
sacrarum* is proved by the fact that in two cases it is held
by Romans of senatorial rank (324, 325 of the same man,
72).

The question of the origin and duties of the *praetores* and
aediles sacris Volcani faciundis presents greater difficulties.
There must have been at times as many as three praetors,
for the titles *praetor primus* (306, 373, 432), *secundus*
(341), *tertius* (376), apparently referring to the rank of
the officers, are found. One occurrence of the title *aedilis
secundus* (*EE.* ix 448) proves that more than one aedile
existed. In three cases one man is both aedile and praetor.[8]
The fact that in one instance a boy who died at the age of
four years was *pr(aetor) pr(imus) sacr(is) Volka(ni faciundis)* [9] leads to the belief that the offices were sometimes
honorary during the Empire at least. These praetors and
aediles were frequently men of prominence in the colony,
decuriones, [10] holders of important priesthoods,[11] and, in two
instances, Roman knights.[12]

[7] Cf. 325.

[8] 3, 376; 390 and 391 of the same man.

[9] 306. Cf. also 341 in which a boy of twelve years is *praetor secundus,* and is also a decurion and a Roman knight.

[10] 375, 376, 349, 412, 415. *NS.* 1911, p. 286.

[11] 373, 391. *NS.* 1910, p. 107.

[12] 341, 390 and 391.

There are two main theories as to the origin of these praetors and aediles. Henzen,[13] who is followed by Beloch [14] and by Paschetto,[15] believed that they were the original magistrates of the colony and that, after they were replaced by *duumviri* and *aediles,* the former magistrates survived and were connected with the religious rites of Vulcan, the chief god of the city. Mommsen,[16] on the other hand, held the theory that these officers were from the first religious, that Ostia had no independent government of her own for a long time, but was governed directly by Rome, who permitted her to have magistrates *ad sacra.*[17]

Both these explanations assume that the magistrates in question performed the priestly offices of the colony from the earliest times, and that they persisted in this function after the duumviral system was instituted for the civil magistrates. This assumption is quite impossible, however, if Ostia did not become a colony until late in the fourth century B. C. If one remembers that the praetorship was established at Rome in 366 purely as a judicial and military magistracy, one can hardly believe that a colony of Roman citizens founded afterwards, so near Rome, should have employed the praetor's title for the priestly office, or for the combined civil and sacred magistracy. Moreover, it is probable that the duumviral system of magistracies existed at Ostia from its foundation as a colony.[18]

It is necessary, therefore, to find some explanation for these priesthoods which will more satisfactorily fit the conditions that we now believe to have existed in the region in early times.

[13] *Ann. dell'Inst.* 1859, p. 197.
[14] *Der italische Bund*, p. 114.
[15] *Op. cit.* p. 117.
[16] *EE.* III. p. 326; *Staatsrecht*, III. p. 777.
[17] Dessau, *CIL.* XIV p. 4, and Ruggiero s. v. *aedilis* p. 270, state both theories, and come to no definite conclusion in the matter.
[18] See introduction.

It is very likely that Vulcan was the chief god of the
small village which, as we have seen, probably existed in
this neighborhood prior to the foundation of the colony.
This village, established as it was on *ager Romanus,* could
have had no independent municipal organization; yet like
every *pagus* or *vicus,*[19] it must have centred about a common
cult.   The suggestion may be offered that the praetors and
aediles of Vulcan were originally officials of that village,
devoted primarily to the worship of Vulcan, though perhaps
possessing certain supplementary duties.   Parallels may be
found in officials of other *pagi* and *vici.*   The aediles of the
vicus of Furfo, elective officers who were in charge of the
temple of Jupiter Liber, had command of the sacred funds,
and were allowed to impose certain fines at will and to
dispose of temple property.[20]   A reference to *aedilitas ad
deam Pelinam* in a *pagus* near Superaequum (*CIL.* ix 3314)
is significant because here, as at Ostia, the name of the god
is attached to the title of the officer of the *pagus.*   The usual
officers of *pagi* and *vici* were *magistri:*[21] *aediles* are found
occasionally,[22] and an archaic inscription records *queistores*
(*CIL.* ix 3849).   It is true that the epigraphical evidence,
which dates chiefly from the Empire, contains no reference
to a praetor as an official of a *pagus* or a *vicus.*   But many
of the Latin towns had praetors as chief magistrates in
historical times, and if, as seems likely, the Latin tribe
lived originally according to the village-community system,
several of these towns must have sprung from *vici.*   The
use of the title praetor for the chief officer of a small village
near Rome would then have been natural.[23]

---

[19] On *pagi* and *vici* cf. A. Schulten, *Die Landgemeinden im römischen
Reich, Philol.* 53, pp. 629-686.

[20] *CIL.* ix 3513.   In Campania during the first century B. C. the
various *pagi* under their *magistri* even gave games under the care of
the *magistri fani.*   Cf. *CIL.* x 3772 ff.

[21] Cf. Schulten, *l. c.* pp. 641, 665.

[22] Cf. s. v. *aedilis*, Ruggiero, p. 266.

[23] The closest parallel to these officers of Ostia is to be found in

After the establishment of the colony the *praetores* and *aediles sacris Volcani faciundis* probably retained their priestly offices, though the titles were sometimes purely honorary during the Empire. The *pontifices Volcani et aedium sacrarum* were perhaps instituted only after the colony was founded.

It is impossible to determine the nature of the cult of Vulcan at Ostia. Wissowa [24] says, " In Ostia genoss Volcanus eine sehr hohe Verehrung, weil für die Docks und Speicher der Hafenstadt die Feuersgefahr ganz besonders zu fürchten war." But there are no dedications which prove that the god was so worshiped at Ostia, and, furthermore, it is probable that his cult existed before any docks and granaries were constructed. Carcopino [25] sees in the worship " un culte qui plonge par de profondes racines dans le plus lointain passé des origines latines, un culte aussi vieux, aussi étendu, aussi vénérable que celui des Pénates de Lavinium, de la Diane d'Aricie, de Juno Sospita à Lanuvium, un culte, enfin, que Rome conquérante évoqua dans les murs en même temps qu'elle le maintenait en son nom, au mieux de ses intérêts et de son prestige, au pays dont il était originaire." Carcopino is doubtless correct in his view of the antiquity of the worship of Vulcan.[26] It is not impossible that the

the *praetor, aedilis,* and *sacerdos Etruriae,* mentioned in a few inscriptions of the Empire. The *sacerdos* was certainly an old office, but Bormann (*Archäol. Epigr. Mitth. aus Oesterreich-Ungarn,* 1887, pp. 112 ff.) advanced the theory that the aediles and perhaps the praetors were instituted under Augustus. The Etruscan magistrates seem to have officiated at a festival at Volsinii. Unfortunately very little is known of the magistrates. Cf. Ruggiero, s. v. *aedilis,* pp. 269-270.

[24] *Religion und Kultus der Römer,²* p. 230.

[25] *Mél.* 1911, p. 188.

[26] Carcopino's most recent statement is less convincing. Cf. *Comptes Rendus,* 1912, p. 104 (report of the meeting of the *Académie des inscriptions et belles lettres* of April 12, 1912). In speaking of the rôle of Ostia in the Aeneid, Carcopino stated that Lavinium really had nothing to do with the story of Aeneas; it was the city of the *Laurentes*

cult was connected with Ficana,[27] a city at the eleventh mile stone of the Via Ostiensis, said to have been destroyed by Ancus Marcius before he founded Ostia.[28]

During the Empire the cult of Vulcan seems to have declined in importance. Though the praetors, aediles, and pontifices are frequently mentioned,[29] we hear of his temple only once.[30] No dedications to him are known, unless we are to identify with Vulcan the *deus patrius*[31] of 3: Deo patrio Cn. Turpilius Cn. f. Turpilianus aedil. et pr. sac. Volk. fac. sigill. Volkani ex voto posuit. Arg(enti) p(ondo) XV. scr(i)p(tulâ) IX.[32]

and of Latinus. The city founded by Aeneas was Troy, which was situated at the mouth of the Tiber, the site later occupied by Ostia. The cult which was connected with this city must, he thinks, have been, not that of the Penates of Lavinium, but that of Vulcan, as later worshiped at Ostia.

[27] Cf. Livy I. 33; Cf. also the title *magister ad Martem Ficanum* in *CIL.* XIV 309. See p. 43.

[28] The view of Paschetto (*op. cit.* pp. 48 ff.) that the importance of Vulcan at Ostia is to be explained by the fact that he was the most important god of Rome at the time of the establishment of the colony can hardly be proved.

[29] There is no evidence to show how these magistrates were elected. Carcopino (*Mél.* 1911, p. 188) believes that the pontifex was chosen by the *pontifex maximus* of Rome.

[30] The frequent mention of Vulcan in the inscriptions of Ostia led to the identification of the large temple on the high *podium* as that of Vulcan—an identification which Paschetto is as yet unwilling to relinquish. It is however to be noted that according to Vitruvius I. 7, 1, the temple of Vulcan should be outside the city walls—*extra murum Veneris Volcani Martis ideo fana conlocari . . . Volcani vi e moenibus religionibus et sacrificiis evocata ab timore incendiorum aedificia videantur liberari.* Vaglieri (*NS.* 1910, p. 13) believes that the temple of Vulcan is to be looked for in the region to the east where the older city probably lay.

[31] Cf. mention of *deus patrius* in inscriptions of Puteoli, Misenum, and Cumae (*CIL.* X 1553, 1881, 3704), which Mommsen refers to the genius of the colony of Puteoli, and Dubois (*op. cit.* p. 40, n. 1) connects with the genius of the colony of Misenum. The genius of the colony of Ostia may be referred to here.

[32] No statues of Vulcan have been found at Ostia. A bas-relief from

THE CAPITOLINE TRIAD

Ostia, like many other Roman colonies, imitated the mother city by building a temple to Jupiter Optimus Maximus, Juno, and Minerva, the great Etruscan triad who were worshiped on the Capitoline Hill in Rome. The existence of such a temple in Ostia is proved by the inscription (32): Pro salutem ... Aug. ... A. Ostiensis Asclepiades aeditus Capitoli [1] signum Martis corpori familiae publice libertorum et servorum d. d. This temple was probably identical with the temple of Jupiter which Livy (xxxii. 1, 10) tells us was struck by lightning in 199 B. C. One dedication to Jupiter Optimus Maximus was found at Ostia. Compare 23. Iovi optumo maximo ex viso aram aedificavit P. Cornelius P. l. Trupo mesor. prec(ario).[2]

The *Capitolium* at Ostia is probably to be identified with the temple whose high *podium* renders it conspicuous among the ruins of the city.[3] This temple has long been popu-

there, now in the Vatican, representing Vulcan, Ceres, and perhaps Neptune, probably had no relation with the cult of Vulcan at Ostia. Cf. Paschetto, *op. cit.* p. 147.

[1] Paschetto's doubts (*op. cit.* pp. 148, 363) as to whether this inscription is originally from Ostia are hardly justified. Dessau notes that the name Ostiensis Asclepiades is mentioned twice in the *album familiae publicae* (no. 255). Asclepiades was a *libertus* of the colony who belonged to the *familia publica libertorum et servorum*, and presented a statue to that body. It is noteworthy that Q. Ostiensis Felix (73), another freedman of the colony, was *aedituus* of the temple of Roma and Augustus.

[2] Mommsen included this inscription in Vol. 1 of *CIL.* (1109), but he says of it there, fortasse rudis potius quam antiqua.

[3] This identification is favored by Nissen, *Rhein. Mus.* 1873, p. 541; Kuhfeldt, *De Capitoliis imperii Romani*, 1882, pp. 26-27, Van Buren, *Amer. Jour. of Arch.* 1907, pp. 55-56, Carcopino, *Mél.* 1910, p. 403. (Here Carcopino states his intention to publish a study of this important temple). On the construction of the temple see Borsari, *NS.* 1893, pp. 191-193; Paschetto, *op. cit.* pp. 363-364.

larly known as 'tempio di Giove' or 'tempio di Vulcano.'
It has recently been pointed out by Van Buren [4] that the
long base at the rear of the temple was apparently intended
for three cult statues, and that the high *podium,* found also
in the *Capitolia* of Pompeii, Timgad, and Lambaesis, seems
to have been employed in places where the *Capitolium*
could not be placed on a hill as at Rome.   Paschetto [5] notes
that the distinctive feature of the *Capitolium* was not the
high *podium,* but the division of the *cella* into three parts,
of which there is no trace in the temple at Ostia.   But the
curious form of the *Capitolium* of Lambaesis, the *cella* of
which is divided into two parts,[6] is conclusive proof that
there was no definitely established form for the *Capitolium.*

CASTOR AND POLLUX

The temple of Castor and Pollux was restored by the
second P. Lucilius Gamala: 376[13] idem aedem Castoris et
Pollucis rest.   An hexameter inscription set up by Catius
Sabinus records the dedication in front of this temple of
a relief or a painting representing games which had been
held in honor of Neptune and Castor and Pollux:

1. Litoribus vestris quoniam certamin[a] laetum
    Exhibuisse iuvat, Castor venerandeque Pollux,
    Munere pro tanto faciem certaminis ipsam,
    Magna Iovis proles, vestra pro sede locavi
    Urbanis Catius gaudens me fascibus auctum
    Neptunoque patri ludos fecisse Sabinus.

Catius Sabinus was *consul II ordinarius* in 216 A. D.   He
celebrated these games as urban praetor (*urbanis fascibus*

---

[4] *L. c.*

[5] *Op. cit.* p. 363 and n. 3.

[6] Cf. Gsell, *Monuments antiques de l'Algérie,* I. p. 144.

auctum), an office which he is known to have held from *CIL*. VI 864.[1]

There is also literary evidence for this festival of Castor and Pollux at Ostia.[2] In the *Fasti Silvii* for January 27th—and it is significant that this is the dedication day of the famous temple of Castor and Pollux in the Roman Forum [3]—are the words: *ludi Castorum Ostiis quae prima facta colonia est.*[4] The games are not mentioned in any other calendar, though it is probable that they would have been given in the *Fasti Philocali* if the scribe had not neglected to fill in the data for the last days of January.[5] More definite information is supplied by the *Cosmographia Iulii Caesaris:*[6] [*Tiberis*] *in duobus ex uno effectus insulam facit inter portum urbis et Ostiam civitatem, ubi populus Romanus cum urbis praefecto vel consule Castorum celebrandorum causa egreditur sollemnitate iucunda.*[7] We have seen that on one occasion the urban praetor Catius Sabinus was in charge of these games. It is therefore probable that in the *Cosmographia consul* is a mistake for *praetor,* and that the games were regularly directed by the urban praetor until the late Empire when the city prefect took charge of them.

But it was not only on the occasion of these annual games that honor was paid to Castor and Pollux at Ostia. Ammi-

---

[1] Cf. Dessau on *CIL*. XIV 1; Albert, *Le Culte de Castor et Pollux en Italie*, Paris, 1883, p. 45, wished to identify the large temple on the high *podium* as that of Castor and Pollux. He thought its size and prominent position in favor of the identification.

[2] This inscription is the only evidence that Neptune shared with Castor and Pollux in this festival.

[3] Ovid, *Fasti*, I. 706. Cf. *Fasti Praenestini* for Jan. 27, *CIL*. I [2] p. 232: ae[dis Castoris et Po]llucis dedica[ta est.

[4] *CIL*. I [2] p. 257, 308.

[5] *Ibid.* p. 308.

[6] Often quoted as Aethicus. Riese, *Geographi Latini Minores*, p. 83.

[7] This statement seems to mean that the games were celebrated at Ostia rather than on the island.

anus Marcellinus xix. 10 tells of a sacrifice made in their temple by Tertullus, the city prefect, in the year 359, when storms had prevented the grain-ships from entering the port and Rome was threatened with famine: *dum Tertullus apud Ostia in aede sacrificat Castorum, tranquillitas mare molluit, mutatoque in austrum placidum vento, velificatione plena portum naves ingressae frumentis horrea referserunt.* Such sacrifices were probably not infrequent and seem to have continued until a very late period. Perhaps Pope Gelasius was referring to similar sacrifices within his own memory when he said: *Castores vestri certe a quorum cultu desistere noluistis cur vobis opportuna maria minime praebuerunt?* [8] It is not improbable that it was for such a sacrifice that Claudius went to Ostia in 48. Tacitus says that he went *sacrificii gratia,*[9] while Cassius Dio explains his purpose as πρὸς ἐπίσκεψιν σίτου.[10] This combined evidence suggests that he may have gone to Ostia in circumstances similar to those of the year 359. However, since it is known that Claudius remained at Ostia for some time on this occasion, it is quite possible that his long stay and his sacrifices were connected with the new port which was then in process of construction.[11]

It is apparent from the evidence quoted that the games in honor of Castor and Pollux at Ostia were not a local celebration, but were under official direction from Rome. Furthermore, it is clear that their temple was at times the scene of sacrifices directed by important Roman dignitaries. Even if the fact that the games were celebrated at the port is not enough to reveal the nature of the worship, the circumstances of the sacrifice described by Ammianus Marcellinus make it clear that Castor and Pollux were here

---

[8] Thiel, *Epist. Pontif. Rom.* I. p. 603, quoted by Wissowa, *Religion und Kultus,*[2] p. 271, n. 1. Gelasius was pope 492-496.

[9] *Ann.* xi. 26. Cf. Furneaux's note *ad loc.*

[10] Cassius Dio, lx. 31.

[11] Cf. Dessau, *CIL.* xiv p. 9.

worshiped as gods who had power to calm the winds and allay storms at sea. Such a conception of the Dioskuri is familiar in Greek literature where the twin gods often appear as the special protectors of mariners.[12] Similar passages in Roman literature seem to be a reflection of Greek rather than of Roman feeling.[13]

In the cult of Castor and Pollux at Rome where these gods were primarily the patrons of the knights, they were never, so far as we know, worshiped as gods of the sea. Throughout the Empire dedications to them are rare; [14] not once are they addressed as gods who calmed storms or rescued mariners.[15] They are not known to have had a temple in any other port town.[16] It is true that their statues seem to have stood in prominent places in the harbors of An-

[12] Cf. passages cited by K. Jaisle, *Die Dioskuren als Retter zur See bei Griechen und Römern und ihr Fortleben in christlichen Legenden*. Dissertation, Tübingen, 1907, pp. 6 ff.

[13] Cf. passages cited by Jaisle, *op. cit.* pp. 27 ff. One may well hesitate to be as positive as Jaisle in explaining all these passages as representing Greek beliefs. To be sure the invocations of the Dioskuri in the *propempticon* of Horace C. 1. 3, in Prop. 1. 17, 15 ff. etc. are most probably based upon Greek precedent. On the other hand, when Horace in C. 1. 12—a poem permeated with Roman sentiment—dwells upon the services of the sons of Leda as rescuers of the Roman ship of state (cf. Kiessling-Heinze *ad loc.*, Hiemer, *Rheinisches Mus.* 1907, p. 240), it seems probable that he is using a mode of speech that would awaken associations with Roman rather than Greek worship. Nor is there anything unreasonable in supposing that Catullus C. 4 dedicated the pinnace to Castor and Pollux according to Roman precedent. The worship at Ostia, as we have seen, was a state cult and could hardly have escaped the notice of these poets. Inscriptions may yet be found to prove that the Roman cult of the Dioskuri as sea-gods was not confined to Ostia.

[14] Cf. Vaglieri s. v. Castores, Ruggiero.

[15] The Greek hexameter inscription of the third century from Marseilles, *IG.* XIV 2461 (quoted by Jaisle, *op. cit.* p. 15), in which the Dioskuri are referred to as πλωτήρων σωτῆρες 'Αμυκλαῖοι Θεοί is thoroughly representative of the Greek conception of the gods.

[16] Unimportant dedications were found at Vibo, *CIL.* X 38, and at Chullu in Numidia, *CIL.* VIII 8193.

cona [17] and Puteoli.[18]   This indicates, however, an imitation of the Greek custom of adorning ports with their
statues,[19] rather than a special cult of the Dioskuri at these
places.

Therefore the worship of Castor and Pollux at Ostia seems
to stand alone in the Roman cult of these gods as the only
reflection of one of the most important aspects of their worship among the Greeks.   But it is significant that the cult
at Ostia was fostered by the Roman state and apparently
not by individuals.   The merchants and sailors, although
they constituted a large part of the population of Ostia, made
no dedications to Castor and Pollux, so far as we know.
Not one of the numerous inscriptions for the welfare of the
emperors is addressed to these deities.   Not a priest of
Castor and Pollux is known from Ostia.

We have no means of determining when the worship was
established at Ostia.   The Romans took their cult of Castor
and Pollux from Tusculum, where the powers of the gods
over the sea were probably disregarded.   In the cult as
known in Southern Italy, however, particularly at Tarentum, Locri, and Rhegium, the Dioskuri must have been
worshiped as gods of the sea.   It is quite possible that the
worship was introduced at Ostia from Southern Italy when
Ostia first became a port of importance, about the third
century B. C.

[17] In the view of the harbor of Ancona on the column of Trajan
statues of Castor and Pollux stand on an arch.   Cf. Cichorius, *Die
Reliefs der Trajansäule*, Vol. III. p. 18, Taf. LVIII; Strong, *Roman
Sculpture*, Pl. LVI.

[18] In the representation of the port of Puteoli on the vase of Odemira
the two figures standing on high columns are almost certainly Castor
and Pollux.   Cf. Dubois, *op. cit.* Fig. 7, pp. 198 f.

[19] Cf. Bethe s. v. Dioskuri, Pauly-Wissowa, col. 1096.   Similarly a
statue of Neptune stood in the port of Claudius, though there is no
evidence for the cult of Neptune at Ostia or at Portus.

LIBER PATER

At Ostia Liber Pater is represented only by a dedication found in the Casino del Sale: *EE.* vii 1195. Sacrum Liber[o Patri?] C. Nasennius Hi[larus] sua [pe]cunia fec[it ob] mer[ita in] Ulpianum f[il e]t ob ṃ memoria[m fi]li sui.

At Portus, however, his cult was very important in the time of Commodus and later. His temple is probably to be identified with a small round Corinthian structure uncovered just to the north of the Casino Torlonia.[1] Nothing remains of it today. The basis for this identification is the inscription (30), found in or near the ruins of the temple: Pro salute imp. M. Aureli Commodi Antonini Aug. Pii Felicis Libero Patri Commodiano sacrum Iunia Marciane ex voto fecit.

Three other dedications to the god were found at Portus: 27. Libero Patr[i . . .] sacrum Chryse . . . 28. Cn. Maelius Epictetus Liberum Patrem in aria sua consacravit. 29. Cn. Maelius Philetus Iun. aram Libero Patri d. d.

Priests and a priestess of the god are known from the inscription from Portus (*IG.* xiv 925): Ἀγνῆς εὐσέμνοιο σπείρης Τραιανησίων οἵδε, ἱερεῖς ἱέρειά τε θεοῦ μεγάλου Διωνύσου Λ. Σούλλιος Λεωνίδης καὶ (vacat) καὶ Ἰουλία Ῥουφεῖνα ἐπὶ παραστάτῃ Σεκούνδῳ.[2]

---

[1] Cf. Lanciani, *Ann. dell'Inst.* 1868, p. 181. " Anche il tempio di Bacco è stato rinvenuto nei recenti scavi al N. del casino Torlonia, là dove vedemmo avere esistito i magazzini vinarii. Esso apparve rotondo, perittero corinzio, rilevato su d'un alto stilobate e risarcito in periodo di massima decadenza. In un frammento dell'architrave curvilineo era scritto a pessimi caratteri: Aur. Rutilius Caecilia[nus]." (*CIL.* xiv 666.) The location of the temple is indicated on Lanciani's plan of the harbor of Trajan, *Mon. dell'Inst.* viii. Pl. xlix. Cf. Altmann, *Die italischen Rundbauten*, p. 69.

[2] *Inscr. Gr. ad res Rom. pert.* i 385; cf. *CIL.* xiv 4. It is not known where this inscription was found, but the fact that it is in the

Another priest of Liber Pater, mentioned in an inscription from Portus, is believed by Carcopino to have been connected with a shrine of the god in Rome. Compare *Mél.* 1909, p. 342.   S]il[va]n[o] sa[cr.] P. Luscius R . . . lanus sacerdos Dei Liberis (*sic*) Patris Bonadiensium Silbano sancto cui magnas gratias ago conducto aucupiorum.   Carcopino [3] compares with *Bonadienses,* which is an ἅπαξ λεγόμενον, the similar forms *Epictetinses, Tellurenses, Orfienses, Caelimontienses,* etc., used in inscriptions of Rome, with reference to the inhabitants of *vici* in the city.[4]   *Bonadienses* are, he believes, inhabitants of a *vicus* which took its name from a shrine or statue of Bona Dea within its limits, and Luscius was the priest of a shrine of Liber Pater in that *vicus*.   Since the organization of *vici* is attested only by one inscription from Ostia which gives the names of *magistri vicorum* (*EE.* IX 470), and since the cult of Bona Dea is unknown at Ostia and Portus, Carcopino thinks that this *vicus* was more probably at Rome than at Portus.   Luscius, he believes, came to Portus because of the hunting,[5] and, after he was successful, recorded his thanks to Silvanus, possibly in the temple of Liber Pater at Portus.

The argument of Carcopino is by no means convincing. There is evidence, not mentioned by him, supporting the natural inference that Portus, as well as Ostia, was organized into *vici*.   Two inscriptions, referring to a σπεῖρα Τραιανησίων (*IG.* XIV 925), Iub. Traianensium (4), prove the existence of *Traianenses* in the port.   It is significant that *Traianenses* are also mentioned in the same fragmentary inscriptions of the city-prefect Bassus in which *Epictetinses, Tellurenses,* etc., are named; they were the inhabitants of a *vicus* of Rome

Villa Albani makes it seem probable that it came from excavations of the Torlonias.

    [3] *L. c.* pp. 343-348.

    [4] Cf. the inscription of the city-prefect Bassus, *CIL.* VI 31893, 31894, 31899.

    [5] See discussion of Silvanus.

which was perhaps in the neighborhood of the Baths of Trajan.[6] Similarly, in the inscriptions of Portus, the *Traianenses* were probably the inhabitants of a *vicus* near the port of Trajan. Since *magistri vicorum* are already known from Ostia, the division of the inhabitants of the port into *vici* can hardly be doubted. Moreover the absence of evidence for the cult of Bona Dea at Ostia and Portus need not deter us from believing that a statue or a shrine of that goddess existed there and gave a name to a *vicus*. In Rome, where excavations have been far more complete than in Portus, it is not possible to explain the origin of all the names of *vici*. Therefore it is not improbable that Luscius was a priest of the temple of Liber Pater at Portus, and that the temple of the god was in a *vicus* of the city, the inhabitants of which were called *Bonadienses*.

A religious association known as a *spira Traianensium* was connected with the cult of Liber Pater at Portus, as is evident from the Greek inscription quoted above. The παραστάς there mentioned is perhaps a magistrate of the body. Many such associations, called *spirae* or *thiasi,* were formed during the Empire.[7] At Puteoli there was a *thiasus Placidianus,*[8] with which a *parastata* [9] seems to have been connected. The association at Portus, like one of the *spirae* at Rome, apparently worshiped Diana as well as Liber Pater.[10] Compare 4 (also found in the excavations of the Prince Torlonia): Diana Tobens. Iub.[11] Traianensium.

A statue of Liber Pater stood in a prominent place in the port of Claudius, if the bas-relief of the Museo Torlonia

[6] Cf. Richter, *Topographie der Stadt Rom*, p. 328.

[7] Cf. Wissowa s. v. Liber, Roscher.

[8] *CIL*. x 1583-1585; Dubois, *op. cit.* p. 134.

[9] *CIL*. x 1584.

[10] *CIL*. vi 261.

[11] Mommsen (quoted by Dessau) conjectured tub(icen). The connection of the inscription with the *spira* does not seem absolutely certain.

faithfully pictures that harbor.   The bas-relief shows, on the
right, a high pedestal upon which stands a nude statue of
Dionysus of a familiar Hellenistic type.[12]   The god is
crowned with the vine and holds the *thyrsus* and a wine vessel.
Beside him is a panther.   Another Dionysus of exactly the
same type is represented on the prow of the larger boat in
the foreground of the bas-relief, while a head of the same
god adorns the prow of the smaller boat.   Guglielmotti, explaining the enigmatical letters on the sail of the larger boat
as V(otum) L(ibero) (2033), believed that the bas-relief was
a dedication to Liber Pater.   The suggestion, though tempt-
ing, lacks support.

A statue of Liber was destroyed in Portus in the sixteenth
century.   According to Volpi (*Vetus Latium,* XI. c. 2) : hanc
statuam Bessarion Trapezuntius cardinalis Nicaenus, cum sui
iuris fecisset, profani cultus impietatem detestatus in mare
demergi iussit.

The cult of Liber Pater was evidently very prominent at
Portus in the time of Commodus, for in the *pro salute* inscription to that emperor Liber Pater bears the epithet *Com-
modianus* which is given elsewhere only to the emperor's
favorite Hercules.[13]   We may infer from the statue figured
on the bas-relief of the Museo Torlonia, which dates from the
time of the Severi, that the cult remained important during
the years following the reign of Commodus.   Indeed we
should expect the cult of Liber Pater to receive special
support from Septimius Severus who built at Rome a great
temple to Hercules and Liber,[14] the gods of his native Leptis,

---

[12] Carcopino, *l. c.* p. 349, disregarding the evidence for the identification
of the temple of Liber discussed above, sees in the position of the statue
of the god in the bas-relief an indication of the location of his temple.
The statue seems to be represented as standing on the east mole of the
Claudian harbor which, it is now agreed, passed over the summit of
Monte Giulio. Cf. Carcopino, *NS.* 1907, p. 736. The dedication to
Silvanus by Luscius was found on Monte Giulio.

[13] Cf. s. v. Commodus, Ruggiero.

[14] Cf. Cassius Dio, LXXVI. 16, 3.

and had representations of them with the inscriptions *Dis Auspicibus, Dis Patriis,* struck on his coins.[15]

Wissowa [16] has shown that Liber as worshiped at Portus was probably an orgiastic Oriental god who appropriated the name of the established Roman deity. The cult of this god was prominent also at Rome and Puteoli. With it were associated *spirae* and *thiasi* which celebrated mysteries of the god, perhaps not unlike those suppressed in 186 B. C. The importance of this cult in Roman ports and the use of Greek in inscriptions of these *spirae* are further evidence for the foreign origin of the worship.

VENUS, FORTUNA, CERES, SPES

The first P. Lucilius Gamala, who, as we have seen, restored (*restituit*) the temple of Vulcan, also built (*constituit*) temples of Venus, Fortuna, Ceres, and Spes.[1] The temple of Venus was restored by the second Gamala (the word *restituit* is used). There is very little other evidence for these four cults from Ostia—none at all, indeed, for that of Spes.

Other dedications to Fortuna from Ostia seem to have no connection with the temple of the goddess. She is grouped with a number of other deities, among them, Invictus deus Sol, in a dedication discovered recently.[2] From Portus comes the inscription (6): Fortunae domesticae sanctae

---

[15] Cf. R. Peter s. v. Hercules, Roscher, 1. col. 2992-2993; Cohen, *Médailles Impériales,*[2] Septimius Severus, 112-122.

[16] *L. c.* Cf. also *Religion und Kultus,*[2] p. 303; Dubois, *op. cit.* p. 137; *Mél.* 1902, p. 27. Dubois attempts to date the revival of these Dionysiac mysteries at Portus from the term *Traianenses,* which he thinks indicates that the inscriptions are of the time of Trajan.

[1] 375, 376. See p. 14, n. 1.

[2] *EE.* IX. 440. Quoted p. 92.

ara pro salute et reditu L. Septimi Severi Pertinacis Aug.
[et D. Clodi] Septi[mi Albini Caesaris] L. Valerius Fronti-
nus ɔ coh. II. vigil. sua pecunia posuit cum suis etc.   In
the latrina of the barracks of the *vigiles* a small shrine of
Fortuna Sancta was discovered.   On a marble *cippus* which
was affixed to the pavement of the room was the inscription
(*NS.* 1911, p. 209): C. Valerius Myron b(ene)f(iciarius)
pr(aefecti) coh(ortis) III. vig(ilum) Fortunae Sanctae v. s.
l. a.   Here too on an *aedicula* which was affixed to the wall
was found the inscription (*ibid.* p. 210), Fortunae sanct.
Vaglieri has noted that this discovery proves that a passage in Clement of Alexandria is to be taken literally.
(*Protrept.* iv. 51).[3]

Ceres, who was naturally looked to as the protectress of
the grain industry, was worshiped by several of the *collegia*.
The measurers of grain were called *mensores frumentarii
Cereris Aug.* (409).   *Quinquennales* of three related colleges dedicated a marble well-head to Ceres and the Nymphs:
2. Monitu sanctissimae Cereris et Nympharum hic puteus
factus omni sumptu. C. Caecili Onesimi patro. et qq.
p(er)p(etui) c(orporis) m(ensorum) adiutor. et L. Hor-
tensi Galli qq. nauticariorum et N. Treboni Eutychetis qq.
II. acceptorum. (consular date 197 A. D.).   Lanciani[4]
suggested that, since the Forum seems to have been sur-
rounded with the offices of corporations devoted to the grain
industry, the temple in the centre of the Forum may have

---

[3] Three statues of Fortuna have been found at Ostia.   One, discovered
by Fagan near the Torre Bovacciana, is now in the Vatican.   Cf. Amelung, *Sc. des Vat. Mus.* Vol. i. p. 101, Braccio Nuovo 86.   For the
second cf. *NS.* 1888, p. 739 and Paschetto, *op. cit.* p. 153, Fig. 26.
Another statue is cited p. 152.   On one of the walls in the so-called
headquarters of *mensores* near the large temple is a small *aedicula* in
which there is a representation of Fortuna, who was doubtless looked
to as the protectress of the grain merchants.   Cf. Paschetto, *op. cit.*
p. 316, Fig. 77; Carcopino, *Mél.* 1910, p. 426.

[4] *NS.* 1881, p. 114.   Excavations now in progress at this temple may
settle its identity.

been that of Ceres. There seems, however, little ground for the identification.[5]

Inscriptions record the dedication of a statue of Venus to Isis and Bubastis (21 add.), and the erection of a statue of the goddess on the sarcophagus of a young girl, Arria Maximina (610). Several statues of Venus have been found at Ostia, among which may be mentioned the beautiful Townley Venus of the British Museum.[6]

But there is evidence for the identification of the temple of Venus which the first Gamala *constituit* and the second *restituit*. A marble altar bearing the inscription (4127) Veneri sacrum was found in a small temple near the theatre. This temple is on the same base with three other temples of almost equal size.[7] Van Buren [8] and, more recently, Carcopino [9] have suggested that these three shrines are to be identified as those of Fortuna, Ceres, and Spes which are mentioned in the same terms as the temple of Venus in the inscription of the first P. Lucilius Gamala. Van Buren, who follows Mommsen in believing that 375 and 376 refer to one man who lived in the time of Hadrian, thinks that *constituit* of 375 is equivalent to *restituit* of 376. From the style of the construction of the temples he comes to the conclusion that they were built in the first century B. C. and restored in the second century after Christ. Carcopino, who dates the Gamala of 375 in the first century after Christ and the Gamala of 376 in the second century, would distinguish between *constituit* and *restituit* in the two inscriptions; he believes that the temples were built by one man and restored by the other. To his mind the

---

[5] *CIL.* XIV 4146 can hardly be related to the cult of Ceres.

[6] Found by Gavin Hamilton in 1775. Cf. *Jour. of Hellenic Studies,* XXI. p. 316; A. H. Smith, *Catalogue of Sculpture in British Museum,* Vol. III. no. 1574.

[7] *NS.* 1886, pp. 127 and 164; *Röm. Mitth.* I. p. 194.

[8] *Amer. Jour. of Arch.* 1907, pp. 55-56.

[9] *Mél.* 1911, pp. 224-230.

style of the construction is in accord with the view that
the temples were built in the time of Augustus and restored under Hadrian.　He notes that the temples adjoined
a private house, which, he suggests, may have belonged to
Gamala.　Since the publication of Carcopino's article, excavations have laid bare a tufa foundation of republican date
under these temples.[10]　This discovery supports Van Buren's
dating rather than Carcopino's.　Carcopino's suggestion,
however, that the house may have belonged to Gamala is
favored by a fragmentary inscription found behind the
temples: Paren ... Lucil[i]us G[ama]la filius ... f.

This identification does not seem improbable.　The cults
of Venus, Fortuna, Ceres, and Spes were not prominent in
the colony, and the four temples could not have been dedicated to any of the more important gods of Ostia.　Yet if
these shrines are referred to in 375, it is strange that the
list of temples is interrupted by the statement that Gamala
fecit pondera ad macellum.　The excavations at the temples
are being continued, and further evidence for their identification may be forthcoming.

PATER TIBERINUS

It is fitting that there should have been a shrine of Father
Tiber at the river's mouth where the god appeared to Aeneas
and foretold the greatness of Rome.[1]　The sanctuary is mentioned in the inscription of the second Gamala: 376, ll.
14-17.　Idem curator pecuniae publicae exigendae et attribuendae in comitiis factus cellam Patri Tiberino restituit.
Gamala restored this shrine not at his own expense, but

[10] *NS.* 1911, pp. 198-199.　Carcopino published some additional notes
regarding these discoveries in *Mél.* 1911, p. 368.

[1] *Aen.* VIII. ll. 31 ff.　Cf. Carcopino, *Mél.* 1911, p. 155; Wissowa,
Religion und Kultus,[2] p. 225.

from the public moneys. The god is represented in relief
on the altar of Silvanus from Ostia, which may have been
intended originally as a dedication to Pater Tiberinus.[2] On
the coins of Nero which represent the harbor of Claudius a
statue of the god stands at the point where the canal flows
into the harbor.[3]

GENIUS COLONIAE OSTIENSIUM

Two dedications to the genius of the colony are known
from Ostia: 8. Genio Coloniae Ostiensium M. Cornelius
Epagathus curat. Augustal. etc. 9. [Ge]nio [col.] Ostiensis [sa]crum [Ti]motheus ... domus ... posuit. A priest
of the cult was a Roman knight: 373. L. Licinio L. fil. Pal.
Herodi equit. Rom. decuriali decuriae viatoriae equestris cos.
decurioni quinquennali duumviro sacerdoti geni col. flam.
Rom. et Aug. curat. oper. pub[l.] quaestori aer. aedili flam.
divi Severi sodali Arulensi praet. prim. sac. Volk. faciu.
ordo Augustal. optimo civi ob merita. Another Roman
knight, mentioned in the fragmentary inscription *EE.* vii
1227, was probably also a priest of the genius. Compare ll.
6 ff. Eutyche[ti] Iun. eq. R. [sac. gen. ? [1]] col. Ost. flam.
divi Ma[rci] .. sodal. A[rul] etc.

The genius of the colony is perhaps to be recognized in
the male figure which is represented standing on a pedestal
in the centre of the bas-relief of the Museo Torlonia.[2] This

[2] See discussion of Silvanus.

[3] Cf. Cohen, Nero 33-38; Van Buren, *Journal of Roman Studies*, 1911,
p. 194, n. 2.

[1] Lanciani, who first published this inscription, and Dessau do not
fill out this line. Though it is impossible to tell how many letters
are missing, there are certainly enough to make this reading possible.
Moreover there seems to be a marked similarity in the order of the
priesthoods in this inscription and in that of Herodes.

[2] See p. 11. There have been various interpretations of this figure
and of the other male figure on a pedestal to the extreme left of the

figure, which is clad in an *himation* and holds a wreath and
a *cornucopia,* is very similar to that on the coins of P. Cornelius Lentulus Marcellinus,[3] representing the Genius of the
Roman people crowning the goddess Roma.

HERCULES

Hercules is represented by two inscriptions from Ostia.
In one of these he is invoked with Silvanus (17). The
other inscription, [Her]c. August., is on a relief which
represents a head of Hercules.[1] It was unearthed between
the Via della Fontana and the theatre in the excavations
of 1909.

At Portus the cult of Hercules may have been more important, for a *pro salute* inscription to Septimius Severus
whose name is in an erasure, probably of that of Commodus,
was discovered there. Compare 16: Pro [salute?] imp.
... Caes. Aug. Nostri L. Septimi Severi Pertinacis Herculi
numini sancto cum basi marmorata acceptatoribus et terraris
C. Sentius Portesis s. p. d. d.   Another dedication was made
by a soldier: 13. ... Herculi [C]assius Ligus trib. coh.
IIII. vigil. d. d. curam agenti[bus] Valerio Frontin[o ɔ
co]h. II. vigil. et Vario Fuficiano .... rio Leone Aemilio
Catullino .. ɔ agentibus.

According to Fea, a temple which was identified as that
of Hercules, apparently by the discovery of a fragmentary

bas-relief. This second figure is clad in a toga and also holds a wreath
and a *cornucopia.* On his head is a crown which is a small model of
the *pharus* represented in the relief. Henzen suggests that the figure
in the tunic may represent the genius of the port, and the other one
Bonus Eventus (cf. *Bull. dell'Inst.* 1864, p. 221), and Guglielmotti
proposes the Annona and the Genius Abundantiae (*op. cit.* p. 16). The
figure in the tunic may very well be the genius of the port.

[3] Cf. Babelon, *Monnaies de la République romaine,* I. p. 401.
[1] *NS.* 1910, p. 100, Fig. 7.

statue of the god in its ruins, was unearthed in Portus in 1794.[2]   It was covered up, but was excavated a second time in 1867.[3]   Since, however, the inscriptions furnish no proof of the existence of a temple of Hercules, the identification seems very doubtful.[4]

SILVANUS

At Ostia as elsewhere there was no public temple of Silvanus, but small private shrines in his honor were numerous.   Altars were dedicated to him by men from the lower classes who were often members of the *familia Caesaris*.[1]   Compare 49 (Portus).   Silvano sac. T. Flavius Aug. lib. Primigenius tabularius adiutor.   52. Silvano sanc. sac. Dorotheus Aug. lib. proc. massae Marian. s. d. d.   50. Silvano s[ac(rum)] Successus Agathemer[i] imp. T. Cae-

---

[2] Cf. Fea, *Viaggio ad Ostia*, p. 39.   " Gli avanzi d'un tempio d'Ercole furono trovati nel sudetto anno 1794, a piccola distanza dall'orlo del porto, colla statua di lui frantumata, e molti residui di cornici, e altri membri di architettura."   Cf. Nibby, *Contorni di Roma*, II. p. 656.

[3] Cf. Lanciani, *Ann. dell'Inst.* 1868, p. 172.   " Anche il tempio di Ercole chiuso nel perimetro del palazzo fu nuovamente sterrato nel passato marzo, ritraendone rocchi di colonne, capitelli di fino intaglio, e tre basi di m. 0, 90 di diametro."   The temple is not indicated on Lanciani's plan of the harbor, *Mon. dell'Inst.* VIII. Tav. XLIX.

[4] Four groups, representing Hercules with the Thracian Diomedes, with the Erymanthian boar, with Geryon, and with Cerberus, discovered in the excavations of Gavin Hamilton at Ostia, are now in the Sala degli animali of the Vatican.   Cf. Amelung, *Sc. d. Vat. Mus.* II. Sala degli animali, nos. 137, 141, 208, 213, Taf. 34.   Another group representing Hercules and Telephus is in the Museo Torlonia (no. 388).   Cf. Reinach, *Répertoire de la statuaire grecque et romaine*, II. p. 233.   A fragmentary statue of the god is in the Lateran.   Cf. Benndorf and Schoene, *Die antiken Bildwerke des Lateran. Museums*, No. 582.   However, the frequency of representations of Hercules in Roman art makes it impossible to attach any special religious significance to these finds.

[1] Cf. R. Peter s. v. Silvanus, Roscher, col. 863.

saris Aug. ser. [p]aterni vicarius [v]otum posuit. Perhaps
the same Agathemerus made the dedication (48) : Sil[vano]
sac[rum] Agat[hemerus ?] fe[cit ?].   A freedman of a freedman of the imperial household dedicated to Silvanus the
beautiful altar in the National Museum in Rome, which was
found behind the stage of the theatre at Ostia.[2]   On the
narrow upper projection of the front face of the altar is the
inscription (51) : [A]ram sac[omari ad Anno ?] nam Aug.
genio [collegii ?] sacomar; lower down on this face : P. Aelius
Trophimi Aug. l. proc. prov. Cretae lib. Syneros et Trophi-
mus et Aelianus fili; on the lower projection : decurionum
decreto.   The dedication, votum Silvano, is on the narrow
upper projection of the left face of the altar; on the right
face is the consular date 124.   Excellent reliefs representing
Romulus and Remus suckled by the wolf, shepherds and
Pater Tiberinus, Mars and Venus, winged genii, etc., adorn
the four sides of the altar.   Since these reliefs have nothing
to do with Silvanus, and since the inscriptions obviously
occupy spaces which are not suited to them,[3] it seems probable that the altar was originally intended as a dedication
to some other god, perhaps to Mars or to Pater Tiberinus,
who, as we know, had a shrine at Ostia.   The words *decreto
decurionum* suggest that the altar probably stood in some very
prominent place.[4]

Silvanus is grouped with other gods in dedications from
Ostia.   An altar to Hercules and Silvanus, who are often
invoked together elsewhere,[5] was found there: 17. Herculi

[2] Cf. *EE.* IX p. 334.   Lanciani, *NS.* 1881, pp. 111 ff.; Lucas, *Röm.
Mitth.* 1899, p. 220; Ducati, *Mél.* 1906, pp. 483-512; Strong, *Roman
Sculpture*, pp. 241-243, Pl. 73, 74.

[3] Ducati, *l. c.*, thinks that all the inscriptions were cut at the time
that the altar was made except the one to Silvanus which was added
later.

[4] Borsari, *Ostia e il Porto di Roma antica*, Rome, 1904, p. 12, thinks
that the altar may have stood in the temple in the Forum which he
identifies as the temple of Roma and Augustus.

[5] Cf. Peter, *l. c.* col. 853.

et Silvano sa[c.] Ti. Claudius Diadumenus cellarius fe[c.]
Unique is the combination of gods in 20 (Ostia). Pro salute
et reditu imp. Antonini Aug. Faustinae Aug. liberorumque
eorum aram sanctae Isdi numini Sarapis sancto Silvano
Larib. C. Pomponius Turpilianus proc. ad oleum in Galbae
Ostiae portus utriusque d. d.[6]

In one dedication recently found at Portus the god is
addressed in his capacity of special guardian of hunters.[7]

A fragmentary dedication to Silvanus was discovered

---

[6] Von Domazewski (*Silvanus auf lateinischen Inschriften, Philol.*
1902, p. 7 = *Abhandlungen zur römischen Religion*, 1909, pp. 65 f.) cites
these two inscriptions with nine others to Silvanus which were set
up by men connected with granaries or other buildings. He thinks
that just as Silvanus was regarded as *tutor finium* in the country,
so when his cult found its way into the cities:—"Hier wird er zum
Beschützer jener Räume, deren unbefugtes Betreten oder Verlassen er
hindern soll." To us the evidence seems far from convincing, since
in seven of the eleven cases cited by von Domazewski Silvanus is
united with other gods. At any rate the *pro salute* inscription from
Ostia, in which Silvanus is grouped with Isis, Sarapis, and the Lares,
cannot be used as evidence that Silvanus was regarded by the *procurator ad oleum in Galbae* (sc. *horreis*) as the special protector of
the granaries of which he was in charge. The dedication comes naturally from a member of the civil service closely connected with the
imperial administration. Cf. Peter, *l. c.* col. 863-864.

[7] Quoted in discussion of Liber Pater. Peter, *l. c.* col. 843, in his
discussion of Silvanus as god of hunters overlooks this inscription.
The other dedications known seem to have been made by hunters of
wild animals. Carcopino, *Mél.* 1909, pp. 346 f. explains the words
conducto aucupiorum of this inscription as ' pour la ferme des aucupia ';
that is, P. Luscius had for a certain period the right to farm out
bird-hunting in a district which probably included Portus, and, having
been successful in his venture, he expressed his gratitude to Silvanus.
The fact that the dedication is made by a priest of Liber Pater is not
convincing evidence for the assumption of Carcopino that the altar
stood in the temple of Liber Pater at Portus; moreover, Carcopino's
statement that dedications to Silvanus from Ostia stood in the temple
of Isis and in the *Metroum* will not bear close examination. No. 20
may have stood in the temple of Isis, but there is no proof that it did,
and No. 53 comes not from the *Metroum* but from the *schola* of the
dendrophori.

recently in one of the tombs. Compare *NS.* 1910, p. 23.
Silva . . . sac . . . s . . .

There was a statue of Silvanus among the dedications to
the *dendrophori* of Ostia. Compare 53. C. Atilius Bassi
sacerdotis lib. Felix apparator M. d. m. signum Silvani
dendrophoris Ostiensibus d. d.   Silvanus, who was regularly
represented as holding a pine-branch in his hand, is probably
to be regarded as the prototype of the *dendrophori* who carried
the sacred pine.[8]   It is significant that in a dedication from
Rome made by a *quinquennalis perpetuus* to the *dendrophori
Magnae Matris* Silvanus is addressed with the epithet *dendrophorus*.[9]

In a niche of the vestibule of the *Mithreum* near the baths
a mosaic representation of Silvanus was discovered.[10]   The
god is represented standing, clad in a short tunic, with the
skin of an animal over his arm. He is bearded and has
long hair; a blue-green nimbus encircles his head. In his
left hand he holds a branch, in his right a hatchet. On either
side of him are trees; on the left there is a dog and on the
right an altar. Another mosaic figure, first interpreted as

[8] This is the explanation of the connection of Silvanus with the
dendrophori which was proposed by C. L. Visconti, *Bull. com.* 1890,
pp. 21-23. Domazewski, *Philol.* 1902, p. 15, Anm. 146 (= *Abhandlungen*, p. 74, Amn. 11), and Peter, *l. c.* col. 866, accept it. But Cumont
s. v. *Dendrophorus*, Pauly-Wissowa and Waltzing, *Étude historique
sur les corporations professionelles*, I. pp. 251 f., are of the opinion that
the *dendrophori* worshiped Silvanus in the first place and became attached to the cult of Magna Mater at a later period. Aurigemma, s. v.
dendrophori, Ruggiero, p. 1678, thinks that the *dendrophori* were attached to both cults, and makes no suggestion as to which they wor-
·shiped first.

[9] *CIL.* VI 641, cf. 642.

[10] Now in the Lateran Museum. Cf. C. L. Visconti, *Ann. dell'Inst.*
1864, pp. 174 f. Tav. d'Agg. L. M., n. 3; F. Cumont, *Textes et Monuments*, II. p. 241, fig. 73; *The Mysteries of Mithra*, Fig. 17; Benndorf
and Schoene, *Die antiken Bildwerke des Lateran. Mus.* n. 551; Peter,
l. c. col. 837; Nogara, *I Mosaici dei Palazzi Vaticano e Laterano*, 1910,
Pl. LXVIII.

Saturn, but which is more probably Silvanus, is found in the pavement of the *Mithreum* near the *Metroum*.[11] Here the god holds a scythe in his left hand and a spade in his right. The scythe is frequently an attribute of this god, and, though no representation of him with a spade is known, there is enough variety in his attributes to make it seem quite possible that he might sometimes have been portrayed with an emblem so well suited to his agricultural character.[12] Silvanus was especially honored by devotees of Mithras,[13] in whose cult he was identified with Drvâspa.[14]

A *collegium Silvani* existed at Ostia. Cf. 309. Dis manibus L. Calpurnius Chius sevir Aug. et quinquennalis – – idem quinquennal. collegi Silvani Aug. maioris quod est Hilarionis functus sacomari, etc. This inscription together with the inscription on the altar of Silvanus in the National Museum discussed above makes it seem probable that the *Collegium Silvani* may have been connected with the *sacomarium* or public weighing place.[15]

GODS OF COLLEGIA

In addition to the religious *collegia* discussed elsewhere— the *Augustales,* the *dendrophori* and *cannophori,* the *colle-*

---

[11] Visconti, *Ann. dell'Inst.* 1868, pp. 402 ff.; Cumont, *Textes et Monuments,* II. n. 295, pp. 414-418.

[12] Cf. list of representations of Silvanus given by Peter, *l. c.* cols. 825-842. This mosaic is not mentioned.

[13] Cf. Cumont, *Textes et Monuments,* I. pp. 147-148.

[14] A painting representing Silvanus is said by P. H. Visconti (quoted by De Rossi, *Bull. Crist.* 1870, p. 78; 1876, p. 40, n. 1) to have been found in the excavations of 1867-1870 at the entrance to a house in Ostia. Dessau on 54 suggests that the report may be a mistake, since neither the younger Visconti nor Lanciani knew anything of the painting.

[15] Cf. Dessau's note on 309; von Domazewski, *op. cit.* p. 8 = p. 66.

gium Silvani Aug. and the *mensores frumentarii Cereris Aug.* may be mentioned the *cultores Iovis Tutoris*(?). Compare 25. Iovi tutori Q. Veturius Secundus A. Libius Hilarianus quaglator et curator donu daeder. cultoribus.[1]   430 mentions a *quinquennalis* of the *collegium geni fori vinarii.*

The venders of oakum were devoted to the cult of Minerva: 44. Numini evidentissimo Minervae Aug. sacrum conservatrici et antistiti splendidissimi corporis stuppatorum ornatam omni cultu d. d. etc.

Two dedications to genii of *collegia* come from Ostia.   One of them was on the base of a statue of the genius, clad in a toga and holding a *cornucopia:* 10. Genio corporis pell. Ost. qui[bus ex. s. c. coire licet ?] M. Aurel. Lamprocles Aug. lib. pat.... s. p. d. d. d.   The other is a *pro salute* inscription: *EE.* ix 434.   Pro salute impp. Severi et Antonini Augg. et Getae nobilissimi Caes. et Iuliae Aug. m. Augg. et castr. genio saccariorum salarior. totius urbis camp. sal. Rom. Restitutianus etc.[2]

MINOR CULTS

Mars.   Statues of Mars were presented to the *dendrophori* (33), to the *familia publica* (32), and to Isis (*EE.* vii 1194).   Fea reports the discovery at Ostia of a statue of Mars on which was the inscription (31), Marti.[1]   The statue has disappeared.   A dedication to Ma. Victori Patri, made by worshipers of Mithras, perhaps refers to a god of the Persian Pantheon who was identified with Mars (*NS.* 1910, pp. 186 f.).[2]

[1] This inscription was found about five miles from Ostia, but probably came originally from there.

[2] Cf. also 51. − − − genio ..... sacomar.

[1] *Viaggio ad Ostia,* p. 53.

[2] Quoted p. 91.

Among the titles of L. Calpurnius Chius, a prominent citizen of Ostia (309), is *magister ad Martem Ficanum.* No satisfactory explanation of the title has been found. Borghesi suggested that it might be connected with the ancient Latin city Ficana which was situated on the eleventh milestone of the Via Ostiensis and was supposedly destroyed by Ancus Marcius.[3] A good suggestion, which does not, however, account for the meaning of *Ficanus,* is that of Gatti [4]—that *ad Martem Ficanum* is the name of a *vicus* of which Chius was *magister.*[5]

Neptune. Strange to say, there is no evidence for a temple of Neptune at Ostia. The god is mentioned only in the inscription of Catius Sabinus from which it appears that he shared with Castor and Pollux the honor of the national games.[6] His statue appears, however, on the Pharus on coins representing the port of Claudius,[7] and in a prominent place in the bas-reliefs of that harbor in the Museo Torlonia. The well-known Poseidon of the Lateran was discovered at Portus.[8] But these statues do not suffice to prove the existence of a cult of Neptune at Portus.

Apollo. A small statue of the god was recently found at Ostia. On its base was the inscription (*NS.* 1910, p. 23), Varenus Augg. lib. adiut. tabul. f. deo Apollini Vip.

---

[3] *Vide* Dessau on 309. Paschetto seems to think Borghesi's suggestion probable, cf. *op. cit.* p. 55. This explanation is certainly more satisfactory than that of Roscher (s. v. Mars, col. 2428), who thinks that the epithet *ficanus* may imply that the fig tree was sacred to Mars.

[4] *Bull. com.* 1892, p. 372. Gatti makes this suggestion in publishing the inscription *EE.* IX 470, which proves the existence of *magistri vicorum* at Ostia.

[5] The famous altar of the National Museum which is dedicated to Silvanus may have been intended originally as a dedication to Mars, to whom some of the reliefs relate. See discussion of Silvanus.

[6] Cf. 1 and see discussion of Castor and Pollux.

[7] Cf. Cohen, *Médailles impériales,* I. Nero 33-41.

[8] The statue was found in the remains of a large building, supposed to be Baths. Cf. Benndorf and Schoene, *Die antiken Bildwerke des Lateran. Museums,* p. 182, no. 287.

Diana seems to have been worshiped by the *spira Traia-nensium*, which was devoted primarily to the cult of Liber Pater (4).

Nymphs. Two dedications to the Nymphs come from Ostia: 46a. Nymphis divinis sacravit D. Hostius Heraclida. *EE.* IX 438. Numfabus (*sic*) Titus Aminnericus donum fecit. A marble well-head was dedicated to Ceres and the Nymphs—a combination not found elsewhere (2).

Deified Abstractions. A statue of Fides was presented, apparently, to the *collegium fabrum tignuariorum:* 5. P. Cornelius Thallus P. Corneli Architecti fil. mag. quinq. coll. fabr. tignar. lustri XXVII. nomine P. Corneli Architecti-ani fil. sui allecti in ordinem decurion. Fidei signum dono dedit. *Tutela* is one of the deities addressed in a dedica-tion [9] found at Ostia.[10]

Dedications to Genii: 7. Genio kastrorum peregrinor. Optatianus et Pudens frumm. fratres ministerio . . . . vota solverunt. 11. Genio loci. On a travertine block recently found is the inscription (*NS.* 1910, p. 31), G(enio) p(opuli) R(omani) f(eliciter).[11]

Domina. It is not known what goddess is addressed in the inscription (74): Thiasus Acili Glabrion. inperatu aram fecit dominae.[12]

Sodalis Arulensis. Four inscriptions of Ostia mention this priesthood, which is not known elsewhere: 341. Me-moriae M. Corneli M. f. Pal. Valeriani Epagathiani eq. [R.] decurioni splendidissimae coloniae Os[tiensis] flamini praetori II. sacra Volkani [fac. ei]demque sodale Arulen[si] etc.   373. L. Licinio L. fil. Pal. Herodi equit. Rom. decu-

---

[9] *EE.* IX 440. Quoted p. 92.

[10] Under the cult of the emperors will be discussed dedications to Victoria Augustor(um), Salus Caesaris Aug. and a possible reference to Annona Aug.

[11] For other cases of this inscription see Cesano in Ruggiero s. v. genius, p. 468.

[12] Cf. Peter s. v. Domina, Roscher.

riali decuriae viatoriae equestris cos. decurioni quinquennali duumviro sacerdoti geni col. flam. Rom. et Aug. curat. oper. publ. quaestori aer. aedili flam. divi Severi sodali Arulensi praet. prim. sac. Volk. faciu. ordo Augustal. optimo civi ob merita. 432. [D.] m. [Q. Vetu]rio Firmio [Felici] Socrati [qq. c. p. d]ecurioni [praet. pr]imo sac. [Volk. fa]ciundis [sodali A]rulesium vix. etc. *EE.* vii 1227, ll. 6 ff. Eutyche[ti] Iun. Eq. R. [sac. gen. ?] col. Ost. flam. divi Ma[rci ...] sodal. A[rul] etc. Three of these *sodales* were Roman Knights. The origin and duties of the priesthood are not known. Carcopino [13] compares the title *sodalis Cabensis,* which is probably a survival of a city Cabe or Cabum which disappeared,[14] and suggests that *sodalis Arulensis* may be evidence for the existence of a city Arula, " une Ostie pre Ostienne." He thinks it may be significant that all of these *sodales* except one are praetors of Vulcan.

[13] *Mél.* 1911, p. 189, n. 2.
[14] Cf. Wissowa s. v. *Cabenses sacerdotes,* Pauly-Wissowa.

CHAPTER II

The Cult of the Emperors

Contact with the Orient, where worship of the emperors had its origin, was probably responsible for the early introduction of the imperial cult at Ostia and at Puteoli.[1] The latter city, Rome's chief port at the beginning of the Empire, had a temple of Augustus built during the lifetime of the first emperor. Ostia, too, though far less important at that time, had a temple of Roma and Augustus which was established before the death of Augustus.[2] This temple must

[1] Dubois, *op. cit.* p. 145. Dubois goes too far when he says of the imperial cult at Puteoli, " L'extension qu'il prit très vite, à cause du caractère oriental de la ville, est confirmée par les nationalités des Augustales .. presque tous portent des noms grecs et orientaux." The *Augustales* were usually freedmen, and Greek and Oriental names are very common among them. It is doubtful whether there are any more such names at Puteoli than elsewhere.

[2] Cf. Hubert Heinen, *Zur Begründung des römischen Kaiserkultes, Klio*, 1911, pp. 129 ff. especially the list of " Priester, Altäre und Tempel des lebenden Augustus in Italien," p. 175. This list includes places where the cult of Augustus alone or the cult of the emperor with the goddess Roma is known to have existed, and Heinen does not distinguish between the two. Inscriptions show that in the lifetime of Augustus Roma and Augustus were worshiped together in Cisalpine Gaul at Pola, Verona, and Tridentum (not mentioned by Heinen, cf. *CIL.* v 5036, cf. also *CIL.* v 5511 sacerdos Romae et Augusti from an unknown place) ; in Italy proper this cult is known only at Ostia, Tarracina, Luna, and Ulubrae (omitted by Heinen, cf. *CIL.* x 6485 which records the restoration of the temple of Roma and Augustus there in 132 A. D.). It is noteworthy that three of these places are ports, where the worship was probably introduced directly from the Orient. A number of the cities in which the cult of Augustus alone was known were also ports—Cumae, Puteoli, Pompeii, Neapolis, Pisae. The lists of places given by Franz Richter s. v. Roma, Roscher, col. 144-145 where there were *flamines* of Roma and Augustus, Roma and divus Augustus, etc. are unreliable. Cf. also W. S. Ferguson, *Legalized Absolutism en route from Greece to Rome, Am. Hist. Review*, Vol. XVIII, 1912, pp. 28 ff.

have been of considerable size, for the *decuriones* sometimes held their sessions there.[3] *Flamines*[4] were in charge of the worship, and an *aedituus* (73), who seems to have been a freedman of the colony, is mentioned in an inscription. Borsari[5] proposes to identify the temple in the Forum, commonly known as that of Ceres,[6] as the temple of Roma and Augustus. Its size and prominent position support the suggestion, but the date of its construction can hardly be placed before the second century. If it were the temple of Roma and Augustus, we should be forced to suppose that it was destroyed at some time and completely rebuilt, an assumption for which there is, as yet, no evidence.[7]

Livia must have had a shrine at Ostia, for a *flaminica divae Aug(ustae)* is known (399, compare 455). There is evidence for *flamines* of the *divi* Vespasian (292, 298, *NS.* 1910, p. 107), Titus (400, 4142), Hadrian (390, 391, 353, *NS.* 1910, p. 13), Marcus Aurelius (*EE.* vii 1227), and Septimius Severus (373). *Flamen*[8] alone, which occurs three times in the inscriptions of Ostia, is probably the same as *flamen divorum*, which occurs once (444). These *flamines* were among the most important men of the colony,

[3] See 353 (inscription of Fabius Hermogenes). Cf. a very similar inscription of the same man found recently, *NS.* 1910, p. 13.

[4] 373, 400, 4142; a *flamen perpetuus* is recorded in an inscription published recently, *Bull. com.* 1910, p. 332.

[5] *Ostia e il Porto di Roma antica*, 1904, p. 12.

[6] Cf. Lanciani, *NS.* 1881, p. 114. Excavations now in progress in the vicinity of this temple may decide its identity, as well as the question of whether it is situated in the main Forum of the city.

[7] There is no evidence for the independent worship of Roma at Ostia. Cf., however, the inscription given by Vaglieri, *NS.* 1910, pp. 104 ff., which records the erection, apparently at Rome, of a statue dedicated to Urbs at the expense of the inhabitants of Ostia. The statue was set up by Ragonius Vincentius Celsus v. c. praefectus annonae urbis Romae. Cf. Wissowa, *Religion und Kultus,*[2] p. 341, n. 1.

[8] 301, 332, 341 and p. 5. Beurlier, *Le culte impérial*, Paris, 1891, pp. 168-172, seems to believe that the simple *flamines* were priests of the reigning emperor.

often municipal magistrates, and sometimes Roman knights
(353, 390). Especially interesting is the dedication which
is on the base of an equestrian statue of Fabius Hermogenes:
353 (restored from the similar inscription, *NS.* 1910, p. 13)
[C. Domitio C. Fil. Pal.] Fabio Hermog[eni] equo publ.
scribae aedil[i.] dec. adlect. flam. divi Hadri[ani] in cuius
sacerdotio solus ac p[rimus ludos] scaenicos sua pecunia
fecit, [aedili]. Hunc splendidissimus ordo dec[urionum
f(unere) p(ublico)] honoravit eique statuam equestre[m cum
in]scriptione ob amorem et industria[m omne]m in foro
ponendam pecun. publ. decr[evit], etc.

Shrines of the individual emperors who had *flamines* probably existed at Ostia.[9] Indeed, remains have been found
of a shrine of several emperors in the heart of the barracks
of the *vigiles,*[10] but this seems to have been a private sanctuary of the *vigiles,* not accessible to the inhabitants of the
city. At the rear of the *atrium* of the barracks, in the
place occupied by the *tablinum* of a private house, a narrow
vestibule opens into a large room. Along the rear wall of
this room is a platform on which are five bases for statues
with inscriptions of the emperors:—(in order from right to
left) Marcus Aurelius before he was emperor (*EE.* VII 1199,
140 A. D.), Marcus as emperor (*ibid.* 1200, 162 A. D.), Septimius Severus (*ibid.* 1203, 195 A. D.), Lucius Verus (*ibid.*
1201, 162 A. D.), Antoninus Pius (*ibid.* 1198, 138 A. D.).
The inscription to Severus which occupies the centre of the
platform is written over an erasure where, as Lanciani has
shown, there was an inscription to Hadrian, in whose reign
the small *Augusteum* was constructed. In the reign of Antoninus, statues of that emperor and of his adopted son Marcus Aurelius were erected, and later, when Marcus was

[9] Perhaps evidence for a shrine of Trajan is to be found in the inscription *NS.* 1911, p. 283. Divo Traiano colleg. fabr. tig.

[10] Lanciani, *NS.* 1889, pp. 72-78. For a view of the shrine cf. p. 74.
plan, p. 78; *Mél.* 1889, pp. 174-179; André, *ibid.* pp. 180-183.

emperor, another statue of him and one of his co-regent
Lucius Verus were added.   On one side of the room is a
base with an inscription to L. Aelius Caesar (*ibid.* 1197,
137 A. D.).[11]   Traces of the sacrificial altar can be seen
in the centre of the room.   On the floor of the vestibule
there is a mosaic representing the sacrifice of bulls, which
Carcopino [12] has interpreted as a group of soldiers sacri-
ficing to a living emperor.

In addition to the worship of individual emperors, the
imperial cult existed in other forms at Ostia.   When the
schola of the *dendrophori* was repaired, it was dedicated to
Numen domus Augustae.   Compare 45. Numini domus Aug.
D[endrophori Ostien]ses scolam quam sua pecunia consti-
t[uerant novis sum]ptibus a solo [restituerunt.   46. Numini
domus Augusti op. pl. p.[13] *EE.* IX 437 Numini domus
Augusti Victor et Hedistus vern. disp. cum Traiano Aug.
lib. a. X. m̊.[14]   A fragmentary inscription (26) seems to
refer to a sanctuary of the imperial Lares.   Compare also
367. P. Horatio Chryseroti seviro Augustal. idem quinq. et
immuni Larum Aug. etc.[15]   Two dedications to Lares may

---

[11] Statues of Severus, Caracalla, Geta, and Julia Domna and of Dia-
dumenianus, Gordian and Furia Sabinia were later placed in the court
outside the *Augusteum.* Cf. *EE.* VII 1204-1211.

[12] *Mél.* 1907, pp. 227-241, Pl. V-VI. André, *Mél.* 1889, p. 182, had
suggested that the name might refer to the cult of Mithras, but Carcopino shows very convincingly that it is far better to explain it as
representing the sort of sacrifice that was probably often made in the
shrine.   The *acta fratrum Arvalium* tell us that a bull was the proper
sacrifice for a living emperor.   All the figures in the mosaic, except
two who are identified as the drover and the *popa,* wear the tunic with
or without the short mantle, and may very well be soldiers.

[13] Non intelligitur (Dessau).

[14] Aeris decem .. ? (Dessau).

[15] The connection of this *sevir Augustalis* with the cult of the Lares
is interesting.   His position as *immunis Larum Aug.* seems to be quite
apart from his rank as *sevir,* though Porphyrio on Horace, *Sat.* II. 3,
281 says that the cult of the Lares was cared for by freedmen called
Augustales.   The evidence seems to show that this statement is wrong.
Cf. Mourlot, *Histoire de l'Augustalité,* Paris, 1895, p. 78.

4

refer to the imperial Lares.[16]   A marble base bears the dedication (68), Victoriae Augustor.   Yet another base, found
recently just outside the city gates, has the inscription:
Saluti Caesaris August. Glabrio patronus coloniae d. d. f. c.[17]
Vaglieri thinks that the inscription dates from the coming
of some emperor to Ostia in the early part of the second
century.   Carcopino tries to date the dedication more definitely.[18]   He notes that a M'. Acilius Glabrio was consul with
Commodus in 186 A. D.[19]   In that year there was a dreadful
plague at Rome, and Commodus, at the advice of his physi-
cians, retired to his Laurentian villa.   Prayers were offered
for the emperor's safety in Ostia, and Carcopino believes
that the statue of Salus may have been set up on this occasion.
The letters of the inscription certainly indicate a second
century date, though perhaps hardly so late a date as the
time of Commodus.   Moreover the base is in close relationship with the second century gate.   But the name Caesar
Augustus should refer to the first emperor,[20] and the simple

[16] 20, *EE.* ix 440.

[17] *NS.* 1910, p. 60.   Vaglieri suggests that the base supported a statue
of *Salus Augusta,* a standing woman about to feed a serpent, of a type
found on the reverse of *denarii* of M'. Acilius Glabrio of 54 B. C.   *Vale-
tudinis* is inscribed on the reverse of these coins, and *salutis* on the
obverse.   Cf. Babelon, *Monnaies de la république romaine,* I. p. 106,
Grueber, *Coins of the Roman Republic in the British Museum,* I. nos.
3943-3946.

[18] Cf. Carcopino, *Journal des Savants,* 1911, pp. 459 ff.

[19] Carcopino states that the father, and probably the mother, of this
M'. Acilius Glabrio were from Ostia.   But his father, who seems to
have been M'. Acilius Glabrio Cn. Cornelius Severus who was consul in
152, was apparently a native of Tibur.   Cf. *Prosopographia Imperii
Romani,* n. 57.

[20] This is the opinion of A. W. Van Buren, *Berl. Phil. Woch.* 1911,
cols. 1390-1391.   For the simple title Caesar used for Hadrian, Carcopino cites the inscription on a brick stamp, *CIL.* xv 4, but the use
of such a title in the limited space of a brick stamp is hardly a
parallel for the use of Caesar Augustus on a large monumental
inscription.

form of the inscription in which the full *cursus* of Glabrio
is not given is an indication of an early date. It is possible that the inscription is a second century restoration of
a dedication from the time of Augustus.

In only a few instances is the epithet Augustus added to
the name of a god, and in no case is it given to one of the
more important gods of the city. Compare 51 [Ann]onam
Aug. *NS.* 1910, p. 100. Herc. August. (found with a
head of Hercules). The *collegia* sometimes gave the epithet to their patron deities. Thus we hear of the *collegium
Silvani Aug., mensores frumentarii Cereris Aug.* A patron
and members of the *corpus stuppatorum* made a dedication
to Minerva Aug. (44).

Augustales and *seviri Augustales* are known in large numbers from the inscriptions of Ostia.[21] Here, as was usually
the case elsewhere, these offices were held by freedmen who
were ineligible to the priesthoods and municipal magistracies. They formed an *ordo Augustalium* [22] which must have
been a very important body in the town. Its officers were
curatores and *quinquennales.* The order seems to have held
slaves who were known as the *familia Augustalium* (367[14]),
and to have had a treasury or *arca Augustalium* to which
members sometimes made gifts (367, 431). There was probably a shrine of the *genius sevirum Augustalium* at their
meeting place.[23] Compare 12. G[enio] sevirum [Augusta-
lium] Ost[iensium] A. Livius ... sevir Augu[stalis cu-
ra]tor annis [continuis ... nom]ine Liviae.

Von Premerstein, [24] who is followed by Neumann,[25] thinks
that it is possible to make a distinction between the *seviri*

---

[21] Lists are given in *CIL.* XIV pp. 573-574. Additional inscriptions
are: Augustalis, *NS.* 1910, p. 187; sevir Aug. *EE.* IX 436; sevir Aug.
idem quinquennalis, *ibid.* VII 1225, 1227; IX 466; *NS.* 1910, p. 107.

[22] 367, 373, 421, 4140.

[23] Cf. von Premerstein s. v. *Augustales*, Ruggiero, p. 853.

[24] *L. c.* p. 851.

[25] Cf. s. v. *Augustales*, Pauly-Wissowa.

Augustales and the *Augustales.* Relying chiefly upon the inscriptions of Ostia for his evidence, he holds that about the year 142 A. D. the *seviri Augustales* throughout the Empire were organized into colleges; that in places like Ostia, Aquileia, and Puteoli, where hitherto only *Augustales* seem to have been known, *seviri* appear and are organized into bodies called *ordines, collegia,* or *corpora,* which succeed the *Augustales.* He dates this organization from evidence which he claims to find in the two following inscriptions of Ostia: 8. Genio coloniae Ostiensium M. Cornelius Epagathus, curat. Augustal. etc. (consular date, 141 A. D.). 33. T. Annius Lucullus VIvir Aug. idem qq. honoratus [26] signum Martis dendrophor. Ostiensium d. d. dedicavit (consular date, 143). He infers from the first inscription that the *Augustales* were still in existence in 141, from the second that the *seviri* were organized by 143. He finds further evidence for this reorganization in the inscription (360): Dis manibus A. Grani Attici seviri Augustali (*sic*) adlectus inter primos, quinquennalis curator perpetus. Rejecting the view of Dessau, who read *inter primos quinquennales,* and supposed that there were different ranks among the *quinquennales,* von Premerstein thinks that Atticus became one of the first members of the order when the *seviri* were instituted about 142.

An examination of the inscriptions of Ostia reveals a weak point in the argument of von Premerstein. He assumes that the phrase *curator Augustalium* in no. 8 could have been used only before the organization of the *seviri,* after which time the *curatores* were called *curatores ordinis Augusta-*

---

[26] Von Premerstein, *l. c.,* expands this as VIvir Aug(ustalis) idem q(uin)q(uennalitate) honoratus; curiously enough, on p. 858 where he cites this inscription among the inscriptions of the *Augustales* and *seviri* of Ostia, he follows the reading of Dessau, sevir Aug(ustalis) idem quinquennalis. The frequency of this phrase in inscriptions of Ostia distinctly favors the latter reading. *Honoratus,* then, probably refers to the college of the *dendrophori,* as Dessau has suggested.

lium.[27] Although there is no other occurrence of *curator Augustalium* in the inscriptions of Ostia, it is significant that in an inscription recently discovered there a *sevir Augustalis* is called *curator eorum,* not *curator ordinis eorum* (*NS.* 1910, p. 107). Moreover, von Premerstein, though believing that the reorganization extended throughout the Empire, makes no attempt to account for the occurrence of the term *curator Augustalium* in an inscription of Puteoli of the year 165 (*CIL.* x 1881). In assuming that in the phrase *curator Augustalium* the plural *Augustales* cannot refer to the organized body, von Premerstein is overlooking the same usage in the phrases *familia Augustalium, arca Augustalium,* both of which occur in inscriptions of Ostia later than 143.[28] Furthermore he neglects the evidence furnished by inscriptions like 367 (182 A. D.) and 431 (about 240), both of whch record gifts of *seviri Augustales* to the *decuriones et Augustales,* who are immediately referred to again as *ordo Augustalium.*[29] An examination of the inscriptions brought together in von Premerstein's lists [30] shows that *Augustales* is frequently used elsewhere to refer to the whole body, especially in such phrases as *decuriones et Augustales,*[31] *arca Augustalium.*[32] In view of these facts we must conclude that von Premerstein is not justified in

[27] Cf. 421, 431. The latter inscription is to be dated about 240.

[28] 367 (182 A. D.), 431 (ca. 240).

[29] In no. 367 the body is referred to as *seviri Augustales* at the beginning (l. 3), as *Augustales* when combined with the *decuriones* (l. 18), and finally as *ordo Augustalium* (l. 20).

[30] *L. c.* pp. 857-877.

[31] This phrase is very frequent, though in many places where it is found, *e. g.* Vibo, Volceii, Atina, Croto, Petelia, the few inscriptions show no cas s of *seviri.* However at Auximum a *sevir et Augustalis* makes a gift to the *decuriones, Augustales,* and *coloni.* Cf. *CIL.* IX 5823. Cf. also *CIL.* v 985 (Aquileia), gift to the *Augustales.*

[32] Cf. *CIL.* IX 491 (Reate). Cf. also *quinquennalis Augustalium, CIL.* IX 2678, 2685 (Aesernia). A *sevir Augustalis* is mentioned in the first inscription, but no *Augustales* are known from Aesernia.

taking 141 as a *terminus post quem* for the organization of the *seviri* throughout the Empire.

On the other hand the inscriptions of Ostia seem to support von Premerstein's *terminus ante quem*. Several of the inscriptions of *Augustales* and *seviri* may be dated approximately by the numbers of the *lustra* of the *collegium fabrum tignuariorum*. Dessau has shown that the thirty-third *lustrum* of this college probably fell between 200 and 240 A. D.[33] By this and other means we are enabled to date the following inscriptions that bear upon this problem:

299. *Augustalis,* before 90 A. D. (2nd *lustrum*)
 33. *sevir Augustalis,* 143 (consular date)
367.   "   "   182   "   "
297.   "   "   160-200 (25th *lustrum*)
EE. VII 1227 *sevir Augustalis,* after 179 (dated from a *flamen divi Marci*)
418. *sevir Augustalis,* 215-255 (36th *lustrum*)
431.   "   "   about 240 (dated from comparison with 352, 432, and 461).

From this list it is clear that *Augustalis* as the title for an individual occurs on no inscription of Ostia which can be dated after the end of the first century, and that *sevir Augustalis* is first found in a datable inscription in 143, and occurs frequently after that. The indications are then that the *seviri* were instituted and formed into colleges between 100 and 143. The fact that *seviri* are far more numerous than *Augustales*[34] is in accord with this conclusion, inasmuch as the number of inscriptions of the first century from Ostia is naturally far smaller than the number for the suceeding centuries. Moreover, *quinquennales* are always *seviri*,[35] that is, they were not known, so far as we

---

[33] Cf. Dessau on 128.

[34] *Augustalis* occurs in 19 inscriptions, *sevir Augustalis* in 64.

[35] The *quinquennales* at Ostia are usually designated by the phrase *sevir Aug(ustalis) idem quinquennalis.*

can tell, before the institution of the *seviri*. Von Premerstein is probably right in believing that A. Granius Atticus
of 360 was one of the first *seviri* elected.[36]

About half of the *seviri Augustales* of the inscriptions of
Ostia are also *quinquennales*. The frequent occurrence of
the *quinquennales* makes it seem probable that the office
became purely honorary, and that the *curatores,* of whom
many are known, were the real officers of the order.[37] This
view is supported by 316. D. m. L. Carullius Epaphroditus
VIvir Aug. idem q. q. – – – Huic VIviri Aug. post curam
quinquennalitatem optuler(unt) qui egit annis continuis
IIII. That is, Epaphroditus was made *quinquennalis* because he had been a good *curator.*

Two *seviri* of Ostia held the same position at Tusculum
(372, 421). L. Antonius Epitynchanus, *quinquennalis collegi fabrum tignuariorum* of Ostia, was *sevir Augustalis* in
Aquae Sextiae (296). On the other hand, L. Numisius
Agathemerus, a *negotiator* from *Hispania citerior,* became
sevir Augustalis at Ostia (397).

Special public honors to members of the order at Ostia
are recorded: 318 D. m. L. Carulli Felicissimi bis(elliarii)
VI [viri] Aug. idem qq. L(aurentis) L(avinatis) qq. cor-
[p]or(is) vin(ariorum) urb(anorum) et Ost(iensium) etc.;
415. C. Silio Epaphrae L. Felici Miori Augustali hunc d.
f. p. efferundum cens. Nerva filius honore usus impensam
remisit etc. 367. P. Horatio Chryseroti seviro Augustal.

---

[36] A further sign of the union of *Augustales* and *seviri Augustales*
at Ostia is found in the fact that in 318 and possibly in 431 *seviri
Augustales* are also *biselliarii, i. e.* they are entitled to the *bisellium*
which is in general the special prerogative of the *Augustales.* The
only other records of *scviri* as *biselliarii* are in *CIL.* IX 3524, 2682.

[37] This is the view of Dessau, *CIL.* XIV p. 5, and of Mourlot, *Histoire
de l'Augustalité,* pp. 117-118. Von Premerstein, however, (*l. c.* p. 852)
takes the view of Schmidt (*De seviris Augustalibus,* 1878, p. 85) that
the office of *quinquennalis* at Ostia was held not for five years but for
one. It is doubtful whether the term *quinquennalis* is susceptible of
such an interpretation.

idem quinq. et immuni Larum Aug. ex s. c. seviri Augustales statuam ei ponendam decreverunt quod is arcae eorum etc.

Members of the order held office in the *collegia:* 309. Dis manibus L. Calpurnius Chius sevir Aug. et quinquennalis idem quinq. corporis mensor. frumentarior. Ostiens. et curat. bis idem codicar. curat Ostis, et III honor., idem quinquennal. collegi Silvani Aug. maioris quod est Hilarionis functus sacomari idem magistro ad Marte(m) Ficanum Aug. idem in còllegio dendrofor. fecit sibi et Corneliae etc. Among the members were *quinquennales* of the *collegium fabrum tignuariorum,*[38] *corpus vinariorum urbanorum et Ostiensium* (318), *corpus fabrum navalium Ostiensium* [39] *corpus treiectus marmorariorum,*[40] *corpus mensorum frumentariorum adiutorum* (4140). In the order was a *stipulator argentarius* (405), and, if one may judge from the reliefs on the sarcophagus of P. Nonius Zetheus, a *pistor* (393).

In the case of at least one *sevir* we have evidence of an interest in literature—that is if we may suppose that Epaphroditus wrote his own epitaph in which a line of Vergil is quoted:—et quem mi dederat cursum fortuna peregit.[41] One is reminded of Trimalchio, the famous *sevir* of Petronius.

[38] 297, 419; *quinquennalis magister,* 418; *magister quinquennalis,* 299, 407.

[39] *quinquennalis perpetuus,* 372.

[40] *patronus* and *quinquennalis,* 425. This is the only *patronus* known among the *Augustales* at Ostia.

[41] 316. Buechler, *Carm. Epig.* 1105, cf. Verg. *Aen.* IV. 653, vixi et quem dederat cursum fortuna peregi. Cf. Mourlot, *op. cit.* p. 123.

CHAPTER III

ORIENTAL GODS

MAGNA MATER

In 204 B. C. the ship which brought the sacred stone of the Great Mother from Pessinus was met at Ostia by P. Scipio Nasica, who had been chosen as the best man of the state, and by the foremost Roman matrons.[1] Here, according to tradition, occurred the dramatic vindication of the noble Claudia Quinta.[2] The ship had grounded at the river's mouth and all efforts to dislodge it were of no avail until Claudia Quinta, with a prayer to the goddess to free her from the false charges that had been made against her, came forward and drew the boat up into the stream.

Although the arrival of the sacred stone must have made a deep impression on the inhabitants of Ostia, there is no reason to believe that the worship of the Great Mother was established at Ostia at that time. Her cult, introduced at Rome by order of the Sibylline Books in order to rid Italy of the foreign foe, was fostered chiefly by the state. It was not until the time of the Empire, when the full Phrygian ritual was adopted, that the goddess made a strong appeal to individual worshipers. At Ostia there is no evidence for the existence of the cult before the second century after Christ. It is possible, however, that it was established there as early as the reign of Claudius when Magna Mater seems

[1] Showerman, *The Great Mother of the Gods, Bulletin of the University of Wisconsin, Philology and Literature Series,* I. Madison, 1901, pp. 225 ff.; Cumont, *Oriental Religions in Roman Paganism,* Chicago, 1911, p. 47.

[2] Ovid, *Fasti,* IV. 305-330.

to have been especially favored at Rome.[3]   There must certainly have been many votaries of the Phrygian goddess
among the merchants who began to come to Ostia after the
construction of the Port of Claudius, and especially after
Trajan's harbor was completed.

The cult of Magna Mater and of Attis who was worshiped
with her became one of the most important of the city.   She
is the only deity except Mithras who is known to have had
temples both at Ostia and at Portus.   *Taurobolia* were performed at both places.   Inscriptions give the names of
numerous priests and devotees of the goddess.   The sacred
colleges which were attached to her cult, the *dendrophori* and
the *cannophori,* had a very prominent place in the life of
the colony.   From no other city outside of Rome is there
so much valuable material, both epigraphical and archaeo-
logical, for the study of the Phrygian cults under the Roman
Empire.

The temple of Magna Mater or the *Metroum* was discovered in the excavations of 1867.[4]   It is situated about
200 yards to the south of the ' *Capitolium* ' and just south
of the Via Laurentina.   It is a small tetrastyle prostyle
structure, with a cella that is almost quadrangular.   Though
no inscriptions were found in it, the finds in the neighborhood identify it beyond a doubt.   Adjoining it was the

---

[3] The March festival of the goddess seems to have been recognized
then, and the cult may have come under the direction of the *quin-
decimviri* at this time.   Cf. Rapp s. v. Kybele, Roscher, col. 1669;
Cumont, *op. cit.* p. 55.   Cf. however, von Domazewski, *Journal of Roman
Studies,* 1911, p. 56, who thinks that this March festival was introduced by Claudius Gothicus.   Wissowa, *Religion und Kultus,*[2] p. 322,
doubts whether the festival was introduced before the end of the second
century.

[4] Cf. C. L. Visconti, *Ann. dell'Inst.* 1868, pp. 362-413, 1869, pp. 208-
245; *Mon. dell'Inst.* VIII. Tav. LX.   The complete publication of the
buildings which was promised by Visconti never appeared.   A small
Mithreum found near by was thought by Visconti to have been a place
for initiations into the cult of Magna Mater.   See also Paschetto, *op.
cit.* pp. 370-384.

schola of the *dendrophori,* identified by an inscription; here
there were two altars, dedicated undoubtedly to Cybele and
to Attis.   In a niche in the *schola* was found a seated statue
of Cybele of about half life size.   The head and fore-arms
were lacking.[5]   In front of the temple was a large quadrangular area, open toward the temple, and shut in on the
other sides by a portico and by rooms opening on the area.[6]
The space was never paved; the ancient level showed a
stratum of fine yellow sand.   The fragmentary inscriptions
(40, 41) found there suggest that the *taurobolia* were performed in this area, which must have been well adapted to
these sacrifices.   There can be little doubt that this was the
campus Matris deum where P. Clodius Abascantus erected
a statue of his son.   Compare 324. P. Cl. P. f. Horat. Aba-
scantiano fil. dulcissimo P. Cl. Abascantus pater qq. II.
corp. dendrophorum Ostiens; (on another side) M. Antius
Crescens Calpurnianus pontif. Volk. et aedium sacrar. statuam poni in campo Matris deum infantilem permisi VIII.
Kal. April. [Plautiano] II. et Geta II. cos. (203 A. D.).
In this area was found the well-known reclining statue of
Attis, now in the Lateran Museum, the best statue of the
god in existence.[7]   On its plinth is the inscription (38):
Numini Attis C. Cartilius Euplus ex monitu deae.   Here
too a bronze statue of Venus, also in the Lateran Museum,
came to light.[8]   Probably this statue was originally either

[5] *Ann. dell'Inst.* 1868, p. 390; Paschetto, *op. cit.* p. 372.   This statue
does not seem to be in the Lateran now.   It cannot be identical with a
colossal statue of Cybele in the Villa Palca, which is said to have
come from Ostia.   Cf. Matz and von Duhn, *Antike Bildwerke in Rom,*
I. p. 241, no. 903.

[6] Visconti, *l. c.* pp. 209 ff.

[7] Reproduced *Mon. dell'Inst.* IX. Tav. VIII. a; Showerman, *op. cit.*
opposite p. 288.   Cf. Helbig, *Führer,* I. no. 721.   The statue is particularly interesting because Attis is represented holding a half-moon,
an attribute of Men, who was often identified with Attis in the Roman
cult.   Cf. Cumont, *op. cit.* p. 62.

[8] Helbig, *op. cit.* I. no. 720; *Mon. dell'Inst.* IX. Tav. VIII.

in the temple, where it may have been dedicated to Magna
Mater, or in the *schola* of the *dendrophori,* where statues
of Terra Mater, Silvanus, and Mars were placed.[9]

Aside from the inscription on the statue of Attis, only one
dedicatory inscription to the Phrygian gods has come to
light: *I. G.* xiv. 913 [θεοῖσι] ἀθανάτοις ['Ρείη τε καὶ "Αττει]
μηνοτ[υράννῳ].[10]

A great many names of priests, devotees, and temple attendants of the cult occur in the inscriptions. Both men and
women were *sacerdotes* of the goddess. The sarcophagus
of one priestess, which is now in the Vatican,[11] has the
inscription (371 add.): D. m. C. Iunius Pal. Euhodus
magister qq. collegi fabr. tign. Ostis. lustri XXI. fecit sibi
et Metiliae Acte sacerdoti M. d. m. colon. Ost. coiug. sanc-
tissime. The inscribed tablet is on the front of the cover
of the sarcophagus. On either side of it lighted torches
are represented in relief; on the left are a *tympanon* and
a *lagobolon,* on the right, cymbals and a double flute, all
objects which were used in the worship of Magna Mater.

Two *sacerdotes* of the shrine of the goddess at Portus are
known from a *cippus* which bears the inscription (429):
L. Valerius L. fil. Fyrmus sacerdos Isidis Ostens et M(atris)
d(eum) Trastib.[12] fec. sibi. The reliefs on this small
cippus, representing a pitcher, two small boxes, a cock, an
hydria, and lotus flowers refer to the cults of both Isis and

---

[9] Cf. 21 add., which records the dedication of a statue of Venus to
Isis and Bubastis.

[10] Omitted by Cagnat, *Inscr. Gr. ad res Rom. pert.* Cf. Drexler s. v.
Meter, Roscher, col. 2919; Hepding, *Attis, seine Mythen und sein Kult,*
Giessen, 1903, p. 82.

[11] Museo Chiaramonti, 179; Amelung, *Sc. des. Vat. Mus.* I. p. 429,
Taf. 45; Altmann, *Architectur und Ornamentik der antiken Sarkophage,*
p. 104. The reliefs on the sarcophagus represent the myth of Alcestis.

[12] M(ater) d(eum) Tra(n)stib(erina) est eadem atque M(ater)
d(eum) m(agna) Port(us) Augusti et Traiani Felicis (n. 408), ita
appellata ab Ostiensibus quod Tiberis inter moenia coloniae et Portum
interfluebat. (Dessau.)

Magna Mater.[13] Compare also 408(a) Salonia Carpime Saloniae Euterpe sacerdoti M. d. m. Port. Aug. et Traiani Felicis patronae suae optimae bene merenti fecit et sibi et Salonio Hermeti Salonio Dorae Saloniae Tertiae et eor. filis pars dimidia intrantib. laeva. (b) M. Cutius Rusticus tibico (*sic*) M. d. m. Portus Aug. et Traiani Felicis fecit sibi et Cutiae Theodote et libertis libertabusq. posterisq. eorum pars dimidia ad dextra.

Archigalli of the colony are mentioned in three inscriptions: 34 . . . . elicis Q. Caecilius Fuscus archigallus coloniae Ostensis imaginem Matris deum argenteam p. i. cum si. gno (*sic*) Nemesem [14] kannophris Ostiensibus d.d. 35. Q. Caecilius Fuscus archigallus c. O. imaginem Attis argentiam p. i. cum sigillo' frugem aereo [15] cannophoris

---

[13] Cf. Benndorf and Schoene, *op. cit.* pp. 52-53, Taf. XVII. 2; Altmann, *Die römischen Grabaltäre der Kaiserzeit*, p. 237, Fig. 191.

[14] *Cum signo Nemesem* (for Nemesis) indicates that Cybele in the statue presented was represented holding a statuette of Nemesis in her hand. Similarly, medallions of Smyrna of the time of Septimius Severus show Cybele holding in her right hand two figurines which represent the two Nemeses whose cult there was perhaps associated with hers. Cf. Decharme s. v. Cybele, Daremberg and Saglio, p. 1687.

[15] *Cum sigillo frugem aereo* obviously corresponds to *cum signo Nemesem* of the preceding inscription. C. L. Visconti, *Ann. dell'Inst.* 1868, p. 393 says " Debbe intendersi che Atti avea, forse in mano, un fascio di spighe, lavorato in bronzo, probabilmente dorato." Dessau finds this explanation unsatisfactory. Cumont s. v. Attis, Ruggiero, points out that *sigillum* must mean a statuette, in contrast to *imago*, the large statue, and thinks it probable that frugem is written for frugis or Phrygis, *i. e.* a priest of Attis. Cf. Dionys. II. 19; Propertius II. 22, 16. The scene would then represent the priest worshiping Attis, a scene similar to that of the woman of the Venetian Bas-relief. Cf. Roscher, I. p. 726. It seems to me more probable that *Frugem* is here a personification—a view suggested by Dessau, *CIL.* XIV p. 565. Attis, who was often represented holding flowers, fruit, and grain as in the statue from Ostia, could very well have been portrayed holding a statuette of *Frux*. However, I know of no such representation of the god. Unfortunately the second volume of Hepding's work on Attis, containing the complete collection of the monuments for the cult, has not appeared. Though there is no evidence for the personification of

Ostiensibus donum dedit. 385 (Small marble *cista* found
in the area described above) [16] M. Modius Maxximus archigallus coloniae Ostiensis. On top of the *cista* there is a
cock. To the right of the inscription are reliefs of a curved
flute and a *pedum;* a representation of a reed pipe breaks
up the letters of the latter part of the inscription. Especially
interesting because of its bearing on the Attis myth is the
relief to the left of the inscription, in which Attis and the
lion of Cybele are represented among reeds.[17]

An *apparitor* of the goddess at Ostia who was the freedman of a priest (probably of Magna Mater) is mentioned
in 53: C. Atilius Bassi sacerdotis lib. Felix apparator M.
d. m. signum Silvani dendrophoris Ostiensibus d.d. The
inscription of a *tibicen* of the shrine in Portus has been
cited.

The title *pater,* which is frequently used to denote an
initiate in the cult of Mithras, occurs at Ostia as the name
of an initiate of the Phrygian cult. With it is found also
the title *mater.*[18] Compare 37. Q. Domitius Aterianus
pat(er) et Domitia Civitas mat(er) signum Attis cann.
Ost. d. d. (On this base are represented a syrinx, a *lituus,*

---

the singular Frux, the plural Fruges, which is more frequently used,
is personified in *CIL.* v 3227 .... elia sacr. Frugibus et Feminis. In
view of the large number of deified abstractions known in later Roman
Religion the deification of Frux seems natural.

[16] C. L. Visconti, *Ann. dell'Inst.* 1869, pp. 240-245; *Mon. dell'Inst.* IX.
Tav. VIII a. 1.

[17] Visconti, *l. c.,* finds in this relief important evidence for the Attis
myth. He thinks that Cybele finally found Attis hiding in thick reeds
on the banks of the Gallos. This would then throw light on the words
canna intrat found in the *Fasti Philocali* for March 15th (cf. *CIL.* I²
p. 260), and on the institution of the *cannophori; * Cumont s. v. *Cannophori,* Pauly-Wissowa, says: "Die Cista aus Ostia ... giebt keinen
sicheren Anhaltspunkt. Es scheint jedoch, dass das Cannophorenfest
an die Aussetzung und Entdeckung des Attis am Ufer des Gallos
erinnerte."

[18] Hepding (*op. cit.* p. 154, p. 187) notes that *pater* and *mater* refer
here to rank among the worshipers of the goddess, rather than to offices
among the *cannophori* or *dendrophori.*

and a Phrygian cap.) 69. Virtutem dendrop(horis) ex arg(enti) p(ondo duobus) Iunia Zosime mat(er) d. d.

Taurobolia were performed both at Ostia and at Portus, and there is evidence for the *criobolium* also at the former place. One inscription, which comes either from Ostia or from Portus, records the performance of the *taurobolium* for an individual: 39. Aemilia Serapias taurobolium fecit et aram taurobolatam posuit per sacerdotes Valerio Pancarpo Idib. Mais. Anullino II. et Frontone cos. (199 A. D.). Three fragmentary inscriptions record *taurobolia* made publicly, probably in every case by the *cannophori* for the emperor and his household, the senate, equestrian order, army, *decuriones* of Ostia etc:[19] 40. Taurob[olium factum Matri deum magn. Idaeae pro salute] Im[p. Caesaris] M. Aurel[i Antonini Aug. et] L. Aureli [Commodi Caes et] Faustina[e Aug. Matris castro]rum libe[rorumque eorum senatus XVvir s. f. equestr.] ordin. ex[ercituum ...] navigan[tium ...] decurio[num[20] col. Ost. ...] canno[phori ...] nat...in... 42. Taurob[olium factum Matri deum] magnae Id[aeae pro salute et victoria] Imp. Caes. C. V[ibi Treboniani Galli Pii] Fel. Aug. et [imp. Caes. C. Vibi Afini Galli] Veldum[niani Vol]usiani P[ii Fel.] Aug. tot[iu]sq. domus divin. eor. [et] sen[atus X]V vir s. f. equestr. ordin. ex[ercituum ....] navigantium s ... 43. Taurobolium factum Matr. deum magn. Idaeae pro salut. et redit. et victor. imp. ... The *criobolium* seems to have been performed under the same auspices. Cf. 41. Crinobolium factum [Matri] deum magn. Ideae pr[o salute] imp. Caes. La ... etc. These sacrifices made by the *cannophori* may be compared with Apuleius' report of the prayers offered by the *pastophori* at the time of the festival of Isis in Kenchreai.[21]

---

[19] Cf. Dessau, s. 40-43. On the *taurobolium* see Wissowa, *Religion und Kultus*,[2] pp. 323-325.

[20] Sacra faciunt cannophori ....; fortasse decurionum quoque mentio eo, non ad formulam voti, pertinet (Dessau).

[21] Apuleius, *Metam.* XI. 17. See p. 71, n. 20.

Taurobolia at Portus, on the other hand, seem to have been performed under the direction of the *archigallus* of Rome, probably on the occasion of the departure of an emperor from there.[22] Cf. Ulpian, *De Excusationibus*.[23] *Is qui in portu pro salute imperatoris sacrum facit ex vaticinatione archigalli a tutelis excusatur.* We have seen that Magna Mater is the only deity except Mithras who is known to have had temples both at Ostia and at Portus. It is possible that her shrine at Portus, with which an area like the *campus* at Ostia for the performance of *taurobolia* was probably connected, was established as a place for sacrifices in honor of the emperors.

The finds at Ostia show clearly the close relation of the *dendrophori* and the *cannophori* with the cult of Magna Mater.[24] Immediately adjoining the rear of the temple of the goddess there is a large irregular room of almost trapezoidal shape which is identified as the *schola* of the *dendrophori* by the inscription of late third century date, (45): Numini domus Aug. d[endrophori Ostien]ses scolam quam sua pecunia constit[uerant novis sum]ptibus a solo [restituerunt].[25] Along the walls of the room, except on the side toward the *Metroum,* is a stone bench spacious enough to provide seating capacity for fifty members of the college. In the centre of the room there were two altars, used, no doubt, for sacrifices to Attis and Cybele.[26] This *schola* must have been adorned with the statues of various gods

[22] Cf. Dessau, *l. c.*

[23] *Fragmenta Vaticana*, 148.

[24] Cf. Cumont s. v. *cannophori, dendrophori*, Pauly-Wissowa, and s. v. *cannophorus*, Ruggiero; Aurigemma s. v. *dendrophorus, ibid.* For a new theory of the origin of the *dendrophori* see von Domazewski, *l. c.* p. 53.

[25] Cf. Hepding, *op. cit.* p. 154, on the connection of the *dendrophori* with the imperial cult in the later period. Cf. also Aurigemma, *l. c.* p. 1704.

[26] Cf. Visconti, *l. c.* pp. 385 ff.; Aurigemma, *l. c.* p. 1679. For plan see *Mon. dell'Inst.* VIII. Tav. LX. B; De Marchi, *Il culto privato di Roma antica*, II. Tav. VI.

which are known to have been presented to the *dendrophori* by members of their body and by devotees of Cybele. Inscriptions record gifts of statues of Silvanus (53), Terra Mater (67), Mars (33), and Virtus (69), to the college. It is not fair, however, to assume from the fact that these statues were presented to the *dendrophori* that all these gods were worshiped by the college. Although Terra Mater, who was sometimes identified with Cybele,[27] and Silvanus were certainly worshiped by them, there is no reason to believe that such was the case with Mars and Virtus. Aurigemma [28] suggests that these gods may have been the special protectors of the persons who dedicated statues of them, or that the statues may have been given simply to adorn the *schola*. Statues of the emperors seem also to have stood there. The bases of statues of Antoninus Pius (97) and Lucius Verus (107) have been found.

Seven inscriptions of the *cannophori* came to light in a niche of this *schola* in the substructures of the temple. Since the *cannophori* are known from an inscription [29] to have had a *schola* of their own, it seems probable that these inscriptions had been removed from it. Two of them are on bases made for statues of emperors.[30] Two others record the presentation to the *cannophori* of statues of Magna Mater and Attis by Q. Caecilius Fuscus, *archigallus* of the colony.[31] A second statue of Attis was presented by two devotees of the Phrygian gods who bore the titles *pater* and *mater* (37). A gift of another statue of Cybele is recorded in 36: Calpurnia Chelido typum Matris deum argenti p.

---

[27] Cf. Graillot, *Mélanges Perrot*, p. 142, n. 7-9. Aurigemma, *l. c.* p. 1678, seems not to know of this identification.

[28] Ruggiero, *l. c.*

[29] Cf. 285. Dessau suspects the authenticity of this inscription.

[30] 116, 117. Cf. 118, 119.

[31] 34, 35. Cumont s. v. *cannophorus*, Ruggiero, suggests that the priests of Cybele and Attis may have held a place among the *cannophori*.

5

II. cantnoforis Ost. d. d. et dedicabit.³² We have already seen that public *taurobolia* were performed at Ostia by the *cannophori*.

In studying the evidence for these two colleges, one is impressed by the fact that statues of the Phrygian gods only were presented to the *cannophori,* while the *dendrophori* received statues of other gods. Perhaps the explanation lies in the difference between the two colleges; the *dendrophori* seem to have been a college that combined professional with religious purposes, while the *cannophori* had a purely religious organization.

EGYPTIAN GODS

The earliest known shrines of Egyptian gods in Italy, the *Sarapeum* of Puteoli and the *Iseum* of Pompeii, date from the second century B. C.¹ The worship was probably introduced at Rome from ports of Southern Italy. As early as 59 B. C. there were many devotees of Isis in Rome,² and the sacred college of the *pastophori* traced its origin to the time of Sulla.³ But merchants from Egypt seem not to have been attracted to Ostia in large numbers before the port of Claudius was built. Indeed the fleet which brought grain from Egypt to Italy (*classis Alexandrina*) probably docked regularly at Puteoli until the port of Trajan was completed.⁴ Later this fleet, which, at least in the early third century, was manned by Alexandrians, brought many

³² Visconti, *Ann. dell'Inst.* 1868, p. 395, notes that *typus* is used to refer to the sacred stone of the goddess which was brought from Pessinus (cf. *Vita Heliogab.* 3, 4), and suggests that Calpurnia gave a facsimile of the sacred stone to the *cannophori*.

¹ Cf. Dubois, *op. cit.* pp. 148 f.

² Cf. Wissowa, *Religion und Kultus,*² p. 351.

³ Cf. Apuleius, *Metam.* XI. 30.

⁴ Cf. Seneca, *Ep.* 77, 1; Marquardt, *Privatleben der Römer*, p. 406.

worshipers of Isis and Sarapis to Portus. A *Sarapeum* was established at Portus by Alexandrians, and modelled after the great sanctuary of the god at Alexandria. Its datable monuments belong to the early third century after Christ. Isis, on the other hand, had a temple at Ostia where she may have been worshiped as a goddess of the sea before there was much direct intercourse between Ostia and Egypt.

The worship of Isis and Sarapis was, as always, closely related at Ostia and Portus. We find at Ostia dedications to Sarapis, and evidence for the existence of a small shrine of Isis at Portus. Bubastis, another Egyptian goddess, shares with Isis one dedication from Ostia. The monuments indicate that the Egyptian gods were most important at the port during the late second and early third centuries, just when their worship was at its height at Rome.

Isis. That the *Iseum,* which has not been definitely located,[5] was at Ostia is proved by the title of the priests of the goddess—*sacerdos Isidis Ostiensis.* Compare 429. L. Valerius L. fil. Fyrmus sacerdos Isidis Ostens. et M. D. Trastib. fec. sibi.[6] 437. D. [m.] M. Ulpi Faed[imi sacer]-dotis Isi[dis Ost?] etc. *EE.* ix 474. D] m. . . . . . . .tiani decur. Ost. [omnib. hon]or. funct. Sal. L. L. . . . . .lic maioris [sacerdo]s Isidis Ost. [incomp]arabilissimo. Compare also *EE.* ix 471. Another priest, probably of the same temple, has the title *sacerdos sanctae reginae:* 352 a. D. Fabio D. filio Pal. Floro Veraiio sacerdot. sanct. reg[in]

---

[5] Paschetto (*op. cit.* p. 401) notes that a number of objects having to do with the cult of Isis were found in the region between the so-called temple of Vulcan and the river, and suggests that the temple of the goddess is to be sought in that vicinity. He enumerates two inscriptions (20, 21), a statue of a kneeling *pastophoros* (present whereabouts unknown), a sculptured pilaster with lotus leaves on it, now in the Lateran (Benndorf and Schoene, *op. cit.* no. 546), and some small fragments of sculpture of Egyptian style.

[6] It is noteworthy that Fyrmus was priest of Magna Mater at Portus. The reliefs on his monuments represent objects connected with the cults of both Cybele and Isis. Cf. Drexler s. v. Isis, Roscher, col. 443.

iudicio maiestatis eius elect. Anubiaco prima dec. Laur. vic.
Aug. Quattervi naviculario V. corpor. lenunculariorum Ost.
honorib. ac munerib. omnib. funct. sodali corp. V. region.
col. Ost., huic statuam Flavius Moschylus v. c. Isiacus huius
loci memor eius sanctimoniae castitat. testament. suo costi-
tui ab heredib. suis iussit patrono munditiario etc.

It was probably a priest of the main sanctuary who with
some initiates restored a *megaron* in Portus. Lanciani has
shown that the *megaron,* known only here in the cult of Isis,
was probably an underground sanctuary designed for the
celebrations of the mysteries of the goddess.[7]   Compare 18.
[Pr]o salute imp. Caes........... p. f. Aug. Camurenius
verv. sac. deae Isidis cap. ced. et ceteri [Isi]aci magar. de
suo restitu.   19. Voto succe[pto] Calventia Severina et Au-
relia Severa nepos megarum ampliaverunt.

From no other place are there so many inscriptions of
devotees and initiates of the cult of Isis and other Egyptian
gods.   Most frequent are the *Isiaci* who, though known from
numerous references in Latin literature,[8] are rarely mentioned in inscriptions elsewhere.[9]   They were initiates of
the cult who were sometimes in charge of a small shrine.
Thus Flavius Moschylus v. c. mentioned in 352 is *Isiacus
huius loci.*   The name of one *Isiaca* is known.[10]   The reliefs
on the sepulchral inscription of Flavia Caecilia seem to
indicate that she too was an *Isiaca,* or, at any rate, that

[7] *Bull. dell'Inst.* 1868, pp. 228 ff.   Lanciani points out that the word
megaron is frequently used to denote an underground sanctuary where
the mysteries of Demeter and Persephone were performed.   The use
of the word *megaron* here in the cult of Isis furnishes additional
evidence for the familiar identification of Isis with Demeter.   Cf.
Drexler, *l. c.*

[8] Cf. Suet. *Dom.* 1; Val. Max. VII. 3, 8; Pliny, *H. N.* XXVII. 53; Min.
Felix 22. 1.

[9] *Isiaci* at Ostia: 18, 343, 352, *EE.* VII 1194.   They are known also
at Pompeii.   Cf. *CIL.* IV 787, 1011.

[10] 302.   Other Isiacae, *CIL.* VI 1780; II 1611.

she made sacrifices to Isis.[11] *Anubiaci,* or attendants who carried the image of the dog-headed Anubis in festivals of the Egyptian gods, also very rarely mentioned in inscriptions,[12] are found at Ostia. A *Bubastiaca,*[13] or initiate of the cult of Bubastis, completes the list of these devotees of the Egyptian gods. The entire absence of evidence for *pastophori* is strange. In view of the prominence of the sacred colleges connected with the worship of Magna Mater, we should expect to find similar organizations in the cult of Isis. It is possible that the discovery of the temple of the goddess will prove the existence of this college.

Dedications from Ostia give further evidence for the cult of Isis. In a *pro salute* inscription (20), she is invoked together with Sarapis, Silvanus, and the Lares.[14] A fragmentary inscription groups her with Sarapis: *EE.* ix 435 Duo v[ir] Isi et S[erapi ta]bernas. In another case she is grouped with Bubastis: 21 add. Isidi Bubas[ti] Vener(em) arg(enteam) p(ondo unum semissem) cor(onam) aur(eam) p(ondo uncias tres scriptula tria), cor(onam) anal(empsiacam) p(ondo uncias quinque scriptula octo) Caltil(ia) Diodora Bubastiaca testamento dedit.[15] Compare also *EE.* vii 1194. P. Cornelius P. f. Victorinus Isiacus et Anubiacus et decurialis scriba librarius col. Ost. signum Martis cum equiliolo Isidi reginae restitutrici salutis suae d. d.

[11] 1044. Flaviae Caeciliae et Q. [M]aeci Iuve[n]alis. The inscription is written on a terra cotta epistyle. To the left of the name of Flavia Caecilia are reliefs of a bull, a *sistrum,* and a basket of fruit; to the right, a bull, a *sistrum,* and a *situla* on which there is a bust, probably of Harpocration. Cf. Benndorf and Schoene, *op. cit.* p. 386.

[12] 352. *EE.* vii 1194. Found also at Nemausus, *CIL.* xii 3043. The title is equivalent to *Anuboforus,* which occurs at Vienna, *CIL.* xii 1919. Anubis seems to have had no separate worship here, but to have been honored with the other Egyptian gods,

[13] 21. Found also at Rome, *CIL.* vi 3880 = 32464.

[14] Quoted p. 39.

[15] Cf. Marucchi, *Il Museo Egiziano Vaticano,* p. 313.

Inscriptions give no information as to the nature of the worship of Isis at Ostia. We do not even know certainly whether she was worshiped in her temple there as goddess of the sea. It is, however, probable that she was so worshiped, since this aspect of the goddess was common elsewhere, and since the annual festival of the Romans which emphasized this side of her cult was apparently celebrated at the harbor.

This state festival, known as *navigium Isidis,* marked the opening of the sea for navigation in the spring. It is recorded under the date March fifth in the *Menologia Rustica* and in the *Fasti Philocali* [16] and is frequently mentioned in the later literature of the Empire.[17] The most important part of the celebration was the launching of a ship dedicated to the goddess. While there is no direct evidence to enable us to determine where this festival took place, it is probable that the Romans celebrated it at the mouth of the Tiber. We have seen that they went to Ostia to sacrifice to Castor and Pollux as gods of the sea, and it is natural that Isis as goddess of the sea should also have been honored there. Compare Lyd. *De Mens.* IV 32. Τῇ πρὸ τριῶν Νωνῶν Μαρτίων ὁ πλοῦς τῆς Ἴσιδος ἐπετελεῖτο, ὃν ἔτι καὶ νῦν τελοῦντες καλοῦσι πλοιαφέσια · ἡ δὲ Ἴσις τῇ Αἰγυπτίων φωνῇ παλαιὰ σημαίνεται, τουτέστιν ἡ σελήνη · καὶ προσηκόντως αὐτὴν τιμῶσιν ἐναρχόμενοι τῶν θαλαττίων ὁδῶν. Apuleius gives us a very minute description of the celebration of this festival at Kenchreai.[18] A splendid procession of worshipers, initiates, and priests went to the sea, and there a beautiful ship, adorned with emblems of the goddess, was dedicated by the chief priest, laden with rich gifts, and launched. Apuleius describes the elaborate procession. It was led by women clad in white garments, some of whom

---

[16] Cf. *CIL.* I,² p. 311; Wissowa, *op. cit.,* p. 354.
[17] Cf. Lactant. I. ll. 21; Auson. *De Fer.* 24; Veget. IV. 39.
[18] Apuleius, *Metam.* XI. 8-17.

scattered flowers and balsam.   Then followed a large number
of devotees of the goddess, both men and women, carrying
lamps and torches.   Pipers and flute-players and a chorus
of youths preceded the initiates.   Temple attendants and
priests of the goddess, bearing sacred symbols and images
of the gods, completed the procession.   We can imagine a
similar celebration at Ostia.[19]   The yearly recurrence of
such a festival may account for the fact that more devotees
of the Egyptian gods are known from the inscriptions of
Ostia than from any other place.   It is noteworthy that the
image of Anubis was carried in the procession at Kenchreai.
At Ostia the *Anubiaci* whose names we know probably carried the image on similar occasions.[20]

Additional evidence that Isis was regarded as goddess of
the sea at Ostia is perhaps afforded by a small bronze lamp
and a wall-painting.   In the recent excavations near the
baths a hanging lamp in the form of a ten-beaked ship came
to light.[21]   On its flat top are reliefs representing Isis,
Sarapis, and Harpocration.   The lamp may have been a
votive offering to the goddess.   The wall-painting, which
was discovered on the Via Laurentina just outside Ostia,
represents Mercury standing beside a ship which is being

---

[19] Dieterich (*Sommertag*, p. 37)) has made the interesting suggestion
that a painting from a tomb near Ostia (now in the Vatican Library)
may represent the *navigium Isidis*.   Cf. Nogara, *Antichi Affreschi del
Vaticano e del Laterano*, pp. 76-77, Pl. XLIX.   The scene represents the
preparation for a festival in which a ship is to be drawn on a cart
by two boys.   In the absence, however, of any of the distinctive emblems of the cult of Isis, it is impossible to come to any definite
conclusion in the matter.

[20] According to Apuleius, ch. 17, after the launching of the sacred
ship, the procession made its way to the temple of the goddess where
prayers were said by a scribe of the *pastophori*—*principi magno sena-
tuique et equiti totoque Romano populo, nauticis navibus quaeque sub
imperio mundi nostratis reguntur*.   The similarity of this prayer to the
form of the records of *taurobolia* made by the *cannophori* has been
noted above.

[21] *NS*. 1909, p. 119, Fig. 2; *Arch. Anz*. 1910, col. 180.

loaded, apparently with grain. At the stern are written the words (2028) *Isis Giminiana,* unquestionably the name of the boat, which may have been a river craft used for transporting grain from Ostia to Rome.[22] Names of gods who had no special powers over the sea were, however, so often given to ships that the name of this ship cannot be considered as strong evidence for the worship of Isis at Ostia as goddess of the sea.[23]

Sarapis. Greek inscriptions, two of which are certainly of the period of the Severi, prove the existence of a *Sarapeum* of considerable importance at Portus:

IG. XIV 914: Ὑπὲρ] σωτη[ρίας] . . . Μάρκου Αὐρηλίου Σεουήρου Ἀλεξάνδρο(υ) Εὐτυχοῦς Εὐσεβοῦς Σεβ(αστοῦ) καὶ Ἰουλίας [Μαμαίας] Σεβαστῆς μητρὸς Σεβ(αστοῦ) Διὶ Ἡλίῳ μεγάλῳ Σαράπιδι καὶ τοῖς συννάοις θεοῖς Μ. Αὐρήλιος Ἥρων νεωκόρος τοῦ ἐν Πόρτῳ Σαράπιδος, ἐπὶ Λαργινίῳ Βειταλίωνι ἀρχιυπηρέτῃ καὶ καμεινευτῇ καὶ Αὐρηλίῳ Ἐφήβῳ καὶ Σ[α]λωνίῳ Θε[ο]δότῳ ἱεροφώνοις καὶ καμεινευταῖ[ς κ]αὶ(?)τῇ ἱεροδουλείᾳ, ἀνέθηκεν ἐπ’ ἀγαθῷ. (On another side) ἐπ’ ἀγαθῷ· ἐπὶ Γρανίου Ῥωμα[νοῦ?].[24]

Ibid. 915: Διὶ Ἡλίῳ μεγάλῳ Σαράπιδι καὶ τοῖς συννάοις θεοῖς τὸ κρηπίδειον, λαμπάδα ἀργυρᾶν, βωμοὺς τρεῖς, πολύλυχνον, θυμιατήριον ἔνπυρον, βάθρα δύο Λ. Κάσσιος Εὐτύχης, νεωκόρος τοῦ μεγάλου Σαράπιδος, ὑπὲρ εὐχαριστίας ἀνέθηκεν ἐπ’ ἀγαθῷ. Permissu C. Nasenni Marcelli pontificis Volcani et aedium sacrarum et Q. Lolli Rufi Chrysidiani et M. Aemili Vitalis Crepereiani IIuir.[25]

---

[22] Now in the Vatican Library. Cf. C. L. Visconti, *Ann. dell'Inst.* 1866, p. 323, Tav. d'Agg. T; Nogara, *op. cit.* Pl. XLVI.

[23] Lucian, Πλοῖον ἢ εὐχαί, describes a large grain ship called Isis, which had been blown from its course on the way from Alexandria to Rome, and had put in finally at the Peiraeus. The name Isis was also given to ships in the Roman navy, cf. E. Ferrero s. v. *classis,* Ruggiero.

[24] *Inscr. Gr. ad res Rom. pert.* I. 389. The *provenance* of this inscription and of the following one is uncertain, but there is no reason for placing them under Ostia, as Kaibel and Cagnat do. They more probably come from Portus.

[25] *Ibid.* 390; *CIL.* XIV 47.

Ibid. 916 : Διὶ Ἡλίῳ μεγάλῳ Σ[αρ]άπιδι καὶ τοῖς συ[ν]-
νάοις θεοῖς τὸν θεοφιλέστατον πά[ππ]ον M. Αὐρ. Σαρ-
[α]πίων παλαιστὴς παράδοξος σὺν τῷ πατρὶ M. Αὐρ. Δη-
[μ]ητρίῳ τῷ [κα]ὶ ['Α]ρποκρα[τ]ίωνι, βο[υ]λευτῇ τῆς
λαμπροτάτης πόλεως τῶν 'Αλεξανδρέων εὐξάμενοι καὶ εὖ
τυχόντες ἀνεθήκαμεν ἐπ' ἀγαθῷ.—Χρυσάνθινα.²⁶

Ibid. 917 :²⁷ Ὑπὲρ σωτηρίας καὶ ἐπανόδου καὶ αἰδίου
διαμονῆς τῶν κυρίων αὐτοκρατόρ(ων) Σεουήρου καὶ 'Αντω-
νίνου καὶ 'Ιουλίας Σεβ(αστῆς) καὶ τοῦ σύνπαντος αὐτῶν οἴκου
καὶ ὑπὲρ εὐπλοίας παντὸς τοῦ στόλου τὴν 'Αδράστιαν²⁸ σὺν
τῷ περὶ αὐτὴν κόσμῳ Γ. Οὐαλέριος Σερῆνος νεωκόρος τοῦ
μεγάλου Σαράπιδος, ὁ ἐπιμελητὴς παντὸς τοῦ 'Αλεξανδρείνου
στόλου, ἐπὶ Κλ. 'Ιουλιανοῦ ἐπάρχου εὐθενείας.

Ibid. 919 : Σερῆνος Ξιφίδιος ὁ κράτιστος νεωκόρος ἐκ τῶν
ἰδίων ἀνέθηκα.²⁹

Ibid. 929 : Σερῆνος νεοκόρος ἀνέθηκεν.³⁰

Ibid. 921 : Σερῆνος ὁ πρεσβύτατος νεωκόρος ἀνέθηκα.³¹

Another *neocorus* of this temple is mentioned in the
Latin inscription, probably from Portus: 188. [Dis mani-

²⁶ *Inscr. Gr. ad res Rom. pert.* 381. Cf. Gatti, *Bull. com.* 1886, pp.
173-180. This inscription was found at Portus.

²⁷ *Inscr. Gr. ad res Rom. pert.* 380. This inscription dates from 201
when Septimius Severus and his train returned to Syria from Egypt.
It was found at Fiumicino.

²⁸ Usually written Adrasteia. She was a Phrygian goddess who from
the time of Antimachos was identified with Nemesis. Cf. Tümpel, s. v.
Adrasteia, Pauly-Wissowa. Nemesis was identified with Isis, especially
at Delos. Cf. Drexler s. v. Isis, Roscher, cols. 543 ff. The statue dedicated to Sarapis by Serenus must have represented Isis as an avenging
goddess. The only mention of Adrasteia in Latin inscriptions occurs
in a dedication to the goddess (whose name is again written Adrastia)
which Steuding s. v. Adrastia, Roscher, and Ruggiero s. v. refer to
some local goddess. Since the cult of Nemesis existed in Dacia (cf.
Rossbach s. v. Nemesis, Roscher, col. 139), it is more probable that
Adrastia is here simply a name for Nemesis.

²⁹ *Inscr. Gr. ad res Rom. pert.* I. 384. Found at Portus.

³⁰ *Ibid.* 391. Found at Ostia.

³¹ Of uncertain origin, but probably from Portus. Quoted by Cagnat,
s. 391.

bus] .. item leg. III I[tal. scribae] [32] aed. cur. sacerd.
bidentali. neocori Iovis magni Sarap. Fundania P. f. Pris-
cilla marito optimo et sibi fecit.

Dessau has proved from these inscriptions that the *Sarapeum* at Portus was modelled on the great sanctuary of the
god at Alexandria.[33] It will be noticed that a senator
from Alexandria made one of the dedications, and that
Serenus, who seems to have been in charge of the Alexandrian fleet, was *neocorus,* apparently at Portus. The form
of address of the god used in these dedications, Ζεὺς ῞Ηλιος
μέγας Σάραπις,[34] and the title of the priests, νεωκόρος τοῦ μεγάλου
Σαράπιδος, [35] are identical with those that occur in the inscriptions of Alexandria. The title ἱερόφωνος is also found
among the titles of the temple attendants of both sanctuaries.[36] Moreover the use of Greek in all the inscriptions
relating to the *Sarapeum* at Portus, except in one sepulchral
inscription, is most easily explained through the close relationship of the shrine at this harbor with the great Alexandrian temple. Shipmasters from Alexandria, who seem
tc have had entire charge of the transport of grain from
Egypt to Portus, probably established and supported the
Sarapeum there.[37] The many temple attendants indicate
that the temple must have been very important in the early
part of the third century.[38]

[32] This is the reading of Villefosse, quoted by Dessau, *EE.* IX p. 335.
[33] *Bull. dell'Inst.* 1882, pp. 152 ff. Cf. s. *CIL.* XIV 47, and Mommsen,
Provinces of the Roman Empire, II. p. 279 and n. 2; Gatti, *l. c.*
[34] Cf. *Inscr. Gr. ad res Rom. pert.* I. 1049, 1050 = *CIG.* 4683.
[35] Cf. *IG.* XIV 1102-1104, for inscriptions of *neocori* of the Alexandrian
shrine found at Rome.
[36] Cf. *CIG.* 4864 = Dittenberger, *Orientis Graecae inscriptiones selectae,*
II. 699.
[37] Gatti, *l. c.* p. 176, believes that the *megaron* of Portus whose
restoration by *Isiaci* is recorded was a part of the *Sarapeum* of Portus.
However the use of Latin in the inscriptions militates against the view.
[38] A leg of a tripod made of red porphyry, found in the excavations
of the Torlonia family, is now in the Museo Torlonia. According to

Dedications prove that Sarapis was worshiped at Ostia also. Two inscriptions in which he is addressed with Isis have been cited above. In the recent excavations between the baths and the theatre the following inscription was discovered: Ἀγαθῇ τύχῃ θεῷ μεγάλῳ Σαράπει Π. Ἀκύλλιος Θεόδοτος ὑγὲρ (sic) Ἀχιλλίου Χρυσάνθους τοῦ υἱοῦ.[39] Since the form of address here differs from that quoted above, it is probable that this dedication belonged to a private shrine, rather than to the temple at Portus.

A statue or bust of Sarapis which stood somewhere near the sea in Ostia plays an important part in the *Octavius* of Minucius Felix. See ii. 4. *Itaque cum diluculo ad mare inambulando litore pergeremus ut et aura adspirans leniter membra vegetaret, et cum eximia voluptate molli vestigio cedens harena subsideret, Caecilius simulacro Serapidis denotato ut vulgus superstitiosum solet, manum ori admovens osculum labiis impressit.* It will be remembered that it was this act of Caecilius which provoked the long argument on Christianity in the *Octavius*. Two busts of Sarapis, a very small one of bronze [40] and another of marble,[41] were found in recent excavations at Ostia.

Bubastis. A dedication to Isis and Bubastis set up by a *Bubastiaca* has been cited.[42] The latter goddess, honored here as elsewhere with Isis,[43] probably had no separate shrine at Ostia, though Ruggiero suggests that an inscription published among those of Rome which mentions a *sacerdos Bubastium* may be from Ostia.[44]

Visconti, busts of Isis and Typhon are represented on it. He makes the suggestion that it probably stood in the *Sarapeum* of Portus. Cf. C. L. Visconti, *Catalogue of the Museo Torlonia*, n. 20.

[39] *NS.* 1909, p. 86. *Année Épig.* 1909, n. 212.

[40] *NS.* 1908, p. 248.

[41] *Ibid.* 1910, p. 63, Fig. 6, p. 64.

[42] 21 add.

[43] Cf. *CIL.* iii 4234.

[44] *CIL.* vi 2249. Cf. s. v. Bubastis, Ruggiero.

SYRIAN GODS

Before the construction of the port of Trajan, the Syrians usually came to Rome by way of Puteoli where they had an important colony.[1] When, in the early part of the second century after Christ, the port of Trajan offered their merchants its spacious accommodations, the Syrians seem often to have found it more convenient to settle at Rome than at the port. In the case of the Tyrians definite evidence on this point is supplied by a letter which their citizens in Puteoli wrote to the mother city in 172 A. D.[2] From this letter we learn that the Tyrians had two warehouses in Italy, one at Puteoli and one at Rome, and that because of their decreasing numbers and wealth, the Tyrians at Puteoli were forced to ask assistance from their fellow townsmen in Rome, in order to pay the necessary rent for their warehouse.

This tendency of Syrian merchants to settle in Rome probably explains why comparatively few dedications to Syrian gods have been found at Portus, and none at all at Ostia, where their merchants must have come in large numbers. There is no definite evidence that a temple of any of their gods existed at either place, though it is not improbable that there was a temple of Marnas at Portus. A Syrian who was connected with a shrine of his native gods in Rome set up an inscription to Jupiter Heliopolitanus. A Roman soldier and a group of Roman mariners made dedications to Jupiter Dolichenus, the god of inland Commagene, whose worship was naturally propagated by soldiers quartered in that region rather than by merchants. Dedications to Dea Syria are unknown at the port. Late evidence proves the celebration of the Syrian festival Maiumas here.

---

[1] Blümner, *Römische Privat-Altertümer*, pp. 624, 633.

[2] *IG.* XIV 830; *Inscr. Gr. ad res rom. pert.* I. 421. Dubois, *op. cit.* pp. 83 ff.

Jupiter Heliopolitanus. The following dedication was discovered in the excavations of the Torlonia family at Portus: 24. I. O. M. Angelo [3] Heliop(olitano) pro salute imperator. Antonini et Commodi Augg. Gaionas d. d. (dated 177-180 A. D. when Marcus Aurelius and Commodus were ruling together). This is certainly the same Gaionas who is mentioned in four inscriptions at Rome, two of which were found recently in the excavations of the shrine of Syrian gods on the Janiculum.[4] From these inscriptions

---

[3] The Latin word *angelus* as an epithet for a pagan divinity is found only here. Henzen (*Ann. dell'Inst.* 1886, pp. 135 f.) thought its use due to syncretism of Oriental religions. Wolff (*Arch. Zeit.* 1867, col. 55) saw the influence of Chaldean star worship in the epithet. A more satisfactory explanation is given by Drexler s. v. Heliopolitanus, Roscher, who compares it with the use of the Greek ἄγγελος in dedications to Διὶ ὑψίστῳ καὶ Θείῳ ἀγγέλῳ. Cf. *Bull. de Cor. Hell.* 1881, p. 182; LeBas-Waddington, *Inscr. d'Asie Mineure*, 416. Here ἄγγελος implies that the god is a bringer of good tidings. Cf. also Gruppe, *Griechische Mythologie und Religionsgeschichte*, II. p. 1323, n. 6.

[4] These inscriptions are: 1) Gaionas' epitaph, *CIL.* VI 32316 (*IG.* XIV 1512, *Inscr. Gr. ad res Rom. pert.* I. 235):

D(is)   m(anibus)   s(acrum)

ἐνθάδε Γαιωνᾶς, ὃς κίστιβερ ἦν ποτε 'Ρώμης
καὶ δείπνοις κρείνας πολλὰ μετ' εὐφροσύνης,
καῖμαι (sic) τῷ θανάτῳ μηδὲν ὀφειλόμενος.
Gaionas animula.

2) *CIL.* VI 420 = 30764 (*IG.* XIV 985, *Inscr. Gr. ad res Rom. pert.* I 70). I. O. M. Heliopolitano Κομμόδῳ ἀνδρὶ βα[σι]λικ[ω]τ[άτῳ] ἀσπιστῇ [τῆς] οἰκουμ[ένης] Imp. Caes. M. Aur. Commodo Antonino Pio [Felici Aug.] Sarm. Germanic[o] trib. pot. x[i] imp. [viii. cos. V. p. p.] M. Antonius M. f. Ga[ion]as Clauc quip .... cistiber dedic. v. c. [a. dcccc]xxxix Imp. Commodo A[n]ton[i]no Pio Felice Aug. V. M'. Acilio Glabrione II. cos. III. k. Dec. (186 A. D.) Gaionas' full name is given only here.

3) A dedication found in the Villa Sciarra on the Janiculum, first published by Gauckler, *Comptes Rendus*, 1908, p. 525. (Cf. Nicole et Darier, *Mél.* 1909, p. 63): Pro salute et reditu et victoria imperatorum Aug. Antonini et Com(m)odi Caes. Germanic. principis iuvent. Sarmatici Gaionas cistiber Augustorum d. d. Gauckler, *Mél.* 1909, p. 243, published his version of the latter part of this almost illegible inscription, as follows: Iovi [opt(imo) max(imo)] Heliopolitano s ... [v?]

it appears that Gaionas was a Syrian, and, judging from his devotion to Jupiter Heliopolitanus, perhaps a native of Heliopolis. He was probably a merchant who had settled at Rome. There he was δειπνοκρίτης, an office apparently connected with the sacred banquets of the Syrian gods in their shrine on the Janiculum. In time he was appointed *cistiber,* that is, one of the *quinque viri cis Tiberim,* a minor office instituted about 200 B. C. which is rarely mentioned. Gaionas, who seems to have been very proud of attaining this position, unimportant though it was, then made dedications to the gods of his native city on behalf of the welfare of, the emperors under whom he held office. He made one of these dedications at Portus between 177 and 180.[5]

Jupiter Dolichenus. Two dedications to the god of Doliche were found at Portus: 22. Iovi Dolicheno pro salute imp. L. Aeli Aureli Comodi Pii Felicis Aug. N. L. Rubrius Maximus praef. eq. alae Hisp. s. votum solvi. This inscription is dated 191-192 by the form of Commodus' name. 110. [Adnuent]e imp. Caes. Com[modo Antonino] Pio Felice sacr(um) qu[od vov(erant) I(ovi) o(ptimo)] m(aximo) Dulic(eno) milit(es) cl(assis) [pr(aetoriae) Mis(enatis) cum es]sent Ostia sub [cura]...ti Iusti tr(ier-

---

1. a. s. [Apro] iterum, Pollione iterum cos. He suggests that the first words may have been Iovi O. M. angelo Heliopolitano, as in the inscription from Portus.

4) An inscription on a block which probably served as a cover of a θησαυρός in the sanctuary of the Syrian gods, found in the Villa Wurts, adjoining the Villa Sciarra; published by Gauckler, *Bull. Com.* 1907, p. 57. Cf. Hülsen, *Röm. Mitth.* 1907, pp. 235 ff.:

Δεσμὸς ὅπως κρατερὸς θῦμα θεοῖς παρ[έ]χοι

ὅν δὴ Γαιωνᾶς δειπνοκρίτης ἔθετο.

[5] It seems impossible to connect this inscription with a departure of the emperors from Portus. Marcus Aurelius and Commodus returned from the East in 176, when they landed at Brundisium. On August 3, 178 they left Rome for the second German expedition, and Marcus never returned. There is no evidence that they went by way of Portus, and in fact their use of this route is improbable. The emperors seem to have remained in Italy from 176 to 178.

archi) VII. id ... [Com]modo Aug. V. cos. [curam agente]
Ter(entio?) Prisco [6] (186 A. D.). Both these inscriptions
date from the reign of Commodus who showed this cult
special favor.[7] It is apparent, however, that neither of
these dedications was made by a permanent inhabitant of
Ostia.

Marnas. The following inscription, said to have been
found at Portus, seems to be the dedication of a statue of
the emperor Gordian III, who had evidently shown special
favor to the city of Gaza during his long stay in Syria: *IG.*
XIV 926. Ἀγαθῇ τύχῃ Αὐτοκράτορα Καίσαρα Μ. Ἀντώνιον
Γορδιανὸν Εὐσεβῆ Εὐτυχῆ Σεβαστὸν τὸν θεοφιλέστατον κοσ-
μοκράτορα ἡ πόλις ἡ τῶν Γαζαίων ἱερὰ καὶ ἄσυλος καὶ
αὐτόνομος, πιστὴ [καὶ] εὐσεβὴς, λαμπρὰ καὶ μεγάλη, ἐξ
ἐνκ[ε]λ[ε]ύσεως τοῦ πατρίου θεοῦ τὸν ἑαυτῆς εὐεργέτην διὰ
Τιβ. Κλ. Παπειρίου ἐπιμελητοῦ τοῦ ἱεροῦ.[8]

The πάτριος θεός here mentioned is Marnas, the chief god
of Gaza. There is no evidence other than this inscription
for the existence of this cult anywhere outside of the Orient,
and even there the worship does not seem to be widespread.[9]
Preller infers from this inscription that there was a temple
of Marnas at Portus.[10] The fact that the inhabitants of
Gaza chose to erect the statue of their benefactor at Portus
rather than at Rome would be most readily explained by
the existence of a *Marnaeum* at the former place. In that
case Ti. Claudius Papirius may have been ἐπιμελητής of
the temple at Portus, though then we should naturally expect
to find the words ἐν Πόρτῳ in the inscription.[11] Ti. Clau-

---

[6] This inscription is cited by Kan, *De Jovis Dolicheni Cultu*, Dissertation, Groningen, 1901, p. 89, and by Cumont s. v. Dolichenus, Pauly-
Wissowa, as from Ostia. The restorations are Mommsen's.

[7] Cf. Cumont, *l. c.*

[8] *Inscr. Gr. ad res Rom. pert.* I. 387.

[9] Cf. Drexler s. v. Marnas, Roscher.

[10] *Röm. Mythologie.* II.[3] p. 399.[2] Cf. Drexler, *l. c.* col. 2382; Cumont,
Oriental Religions in Roman Paganism, p. 243, n. 16.

[11] Cf. *IG.* XIV 914 νεωκόρος τοῦ ἐν Πόρτῳ Σαράπιδος.

dius **Papirius** is, however, more likely to be the name of a
citizen of Ostia than of a citizen of Gaza. Since the latter
city was a *civitas foederata* at the time of this inscription,[12]
its inhabitants must have received citizenship under the
Edict of Caracalla. We should therefore expect to find its
citizens bearing the name Aurelius, and not Tiberius Claudius, which is not found in the indices to the Greek and
Latin inscriptions of Syria. Claudius occurs in the indices
only four times, while Aurelius occurs thirty times. Furthermore the indices of inscriptions from Syria do not contain the name Papirius, whereas the name occurs in Ostia
(1448). The evidence does not, however, justify any
definite conclusion on this point.

Festival of Maiumas. A popular festival known as
Maiumas which seems usually to have been accompanied
by considerable licentiousness was celebrated in various parts
of the Orient, notably at Antioch.[13] Later emperors tried
to control it, and at times forbade it entirely. Inasmuch
as the harbor of Gaza was called *Maiumas,* which means
' water of the sea,' Stark suggested that the celebration origi-
nated there.[14] According to Suidas s. v. Μαϊουμᾶς, a festival of this name was held at Ostia: πανήγυρις ἤγετο ἐν τῇ
Ῥώμῃ κατὰ τὸν Μάιον μῆνα. τὴν παράλιον καταλαμβάνοντες
πόλιν, τὴν λεγομένην Ὀστίαν, οἱ τὰ πρῶτα τῆς Ῥώμης
τελοῦντες ἡδυπαθεῖν ἠνείχοντο, ἐν τοῖς θαλαττίοις ὕδασιν

---

[12] Cf. *Inscr. Gr. ad res Rom. pert.* III 1212 (on a lead weight) Κολωνίας
Γάζης ἐπὶ Ἡρώδου Διοφάντου. (on the side) ιέ. Cagnat suggests that
this inscription may be dated in the fifteenth year of the reign of
Hadrian. He seems, however, to have overlooked the inscription from
Portus which proves that Gaza was a *civitas foederata* in the time of
Gordian III (238-244). It must have been made a colony later.

[13] Cf. articles *Maiumas* by Teuffel, Pauly, *Real Encycl.;* Drexler,
Roscher; Saglio, Daremberg and Saglio. Cf. also Büchler, *Revue des
Études Juives,* XLII, 1901, pp. 125 ff.; Clermont-Ganneau, *Recueil d'arch.
orientale,* IV. p. 339; Abel, *Revue Biblique,* 1909, p. 598.

[14] Stark, *Gaza,* pp. 596-598, quoted by Drexler *l. c.*

ἀλλήλους ἐμβάλλοντες. ὅθεν καὶ Μαϊουμᾶς ὁ τῆς τοιαύτης ἑορτῆς καιρὸς ὠνομάζετο.

The connection of the festival with the month of May and with Maia is obviously a mistaken effort to explain the etymology of the word *Maiumas*,[15] for it is known that the celebration at Antioch took place in August. Teuffel,[16] who is followed by Drexler, doubts whether such a festival was known at Ostia. After recalling the evidence for the games in honor of Castor and Pollux there, Teuffel adds: "Vielmehr scheint Suidas und der Glossator diese ludi Tiberini wegen ihrer Ähnlichkeit mit einem syrischen Feste des Namens verwechselt zu haben und von hier aus auf seine Ableitung des Wortes und auf die Datierung in den Mai geführt worden zu sein."

It is, however, difficult to reconcile the unrestrained celebration described by Suidas with the festival in honor of Castor and Pollux, *ubi populus Romanus – – – Castorum celebrandorum causa egreditur sollemnitate iucunda*.[17] Moreover, in view of the fact that intercourse with Gaza is proved for the time of Gordian III,[18] it seems not improbable that this Syrian festival was introduced at Ostia during the later empire. There is but very slight foundation for the unqualified statement of A. J. Reinach:[19] "La fête de Maioumas s'est introduite à Ostie avec les adorateurs du

---

[15] Cf. also the Basilica glosses, cited by Drexler, *l. c.* Μαιουμᾶς ἑορτὴ ἐν Ῥώμῃ etc. and Joh. Lyd. *De Mens.* IV. 52. Lydus is trying to explain the etymology of *Maius*: κατὰ δὲ τὸν τῆς φυσιολογίας τρόπον τὴν Μαῖαν οἱ πολλοὶ τὸ ὕδωρ εἶναι βούλονται· καὶ γὰρ παρὰ τοῖς Σύροις βαρβαρίζουσιν οὕτως ἔτι καὶ νῦν τὸ ὕδωρ προσαγορεύεται, ὡς καὶ μήτουρι τὰ ὑδροφόρα καλεῖσθαι. *ibid.* IV 53. Lydus is explaining that there is special danger of earthquakes in May: τιμῶσιν οὖν κατὰ τοῦτον τὴν Μαῖαν, τουτέστι τὴν γῆν θεραπεύοντες. μαϊουμίζειν τὸ ἑορτάζειν ὀνομάζουσιν, ἐξ οὗ καὶ μαϊουμᾶν.

[16] *L. c.*

[17] See discussion of Castor and Pollux.

[18] Cf. *IG.* XIV 926.

[19] *Revue Arch.* XV. 1910, p. 49, n. 2. Cumont seems to agree, cf. *Oriental Religions in Roman Paganism*, p. 243, n. 16.

6

Marnas de Gaza." As we have seen, the evidence does not suffice to prove the existence of a cult of Marnas at Ostia.[20]

MITHRAS

Toward the end of the first century of our era the conquests of the Flavian emperors in the interior of Asia Minor brought Rome into contact with a region in which the most important cult was that of the Persian god Mithras. The worship of this god spread rapidly through the Empire, until in the early third century he numbered more devotees than any other pagan deity. The cult of Mithras was propagated in the West chiefly by soldiers, slaves, and merchants. Recruits levied in the lands where Mithras reigned supreme or legionaries who had been quartered in those regions carried his worship to the most distant confines of the Empire.[1] Eastern slaves who were brought in large numbers to Italy and especially to Rome were zealous missionaries of Mithras and many of them continued to propagate his worship after they were freed. Asiatic merchants as well as slaves were instrumental in establishing the cult in the ports of the Mediterranean. It was known in the ports of Alexandria and Sidon in the East, and at Pola, Aquileia, Ostia, Antium, and Rusellae in Italy.[2] That evidence for the worship of Mithras is lacking at Puteoli is at least partially explained by the fact that the Oriental trade of that

[20] As Drexler *l. c.* has shown, the assumption of Preller, *Röm. Mythol.* II. p. 399, Mommsen, *Eph. Epig.* 3 p. 329, and Reville, *Die Religion der römischen Gesellschaft in der Zeit des Syncretismus*, p. 72, that Maiuma is a Syrian form of the goddess Venus is totally without foundation.

[1] Cf. however, C. H. Moore, *Distribution of Oriental Cults* in *Transactions of the American Philological Association*, 1907, pp. 142 ff. The author shows that soldiers were less prominent in spreading the cult of Mithras than has generally been supposed.

[2] Cf. Cumont, *The Mysteries of Mithra*, p. 64.

port decreased greatly after the construction of the ports of Claudius and Trajan.[3]

The form of the temple of Mithras or the *Mithreum* is distinctive. Unlike the Greco-Roman temple which was simply the house of the god, the *Mithreum* was a place where the faithful assembled to worship. The sanctuary was usually small, accommodating ordinarily about fifty people. Whenever the number of devotees exceeded the capacity of a *Mithreum,* a new one was built. It was often an underground chamber and was regularly divided into three main parts. A central portion or choir, usually about two meters wide, where probably the priests alone were permitted, was flanked on either side by raised benches or *podia,* the inclined surfaces of which were a meter to a meter and a half in width. Here the faithful probably knelt during worship. At the further end of the sanctuary there was always a sculptured group representing Mithras slaying the bull (Mithras Tauroctonos).[4]

At least six *Mithrea* are known to have existed at Ostia and Portus.[5] Only at Rome is there evidence for a larger number of shrines. Moreover the excellent preservation of the *Mithrea,* the Mithraic inscriptions, and the statues found at Ostia, and the early date of some of the monuments make the remains exceedingly valuable to students of the cult of Mithras. Probably the earliest *Mithreum* known is the one

[3] Cf. Dubois, *op. cit.* p. 153.

[4] Cf. Cumont, *Textes et monuments figurés relatifs aux mystères de Mithra,* I. pp. 59 f.

[5] Plutarch in his life of Pompey, c. 24, states that Romans were initiated into the mysteries of Mithras by Cilician pirates who had been conquered by Pompey. C. L. Visconti, *Ann. dell'Inst.* 1864, p. 147, recalls Cicero's words (*De Lege Manil.* 12, 33) about the defeat of the Roman fleet by the pirates at Ostia and considers it probable that, after the successful termination of the war, the ships gathered at Ostia, where the soldiers and sailors may have introduced the worship of Mithras. There is nothing to support this view. Subsequent researches have shown that the Persian god could have had very few devotees in the West before the end of the first century after Christ.

84 THE CULTS OF OSTIA

near the *Metroum* at Ostia, which seems to date from the
time of Hadrian. In another temple an inscription of 162
A. D. was found. Since, however, Mithraic inscriptions of
an earlier date have been found at Rome, there is no reason
to suppose that the cult at Ostia antedated that at Rome.

Inscriptions of Ostia give the names of *sacerdotes* and
antistites of Mithras.[6] Some of these priests bear the titles
pater et sacerdos, pater et antistes, which indicate that they
had attained to the highest of the seven degrees of initiation
in the cult.[7] The simple title *pater* is also of frequent occurrence. An initiate who had reached the fourth degree, that
of *leo,* inscribed at Portus a list of the members of an
association of worshipers of Mithras.

The Mithraic monuments found at Ostia prior to 1896
have received exhaustive treatment in the great work of
Cumont: *Textes et monuments figurés relatifs au mystères
de Mithra.*[8] The following discussion has therefore been
confined to a brief summary of the most important finds in
the individual *Mithrea,* together with a consideration of the
inscriptions and other remains recently brought to light.

The temple discovered in 1867 about three meters from
the northeast corner of the temple of Magna Mater is proba-

[6] Cumont, *Mysteries of Mithra,* p. 165, finds no distinction in the use
of the two titles.

[7] *Ibid.* p. 152. Cf. W. J. Pythian-Adams, on *The Problem of the
Mithraic Grades* in *Journal of Roman Studies,* 1912, pp. 53 ff. The
author attempts to show that there were only six grades in the Mithraic
initiation.

[8] Vol. II, 1896, Vol. I, 1899. Vol. II contains texts, inscriptions, and
monuments. Inscriptions 131-142, 560 a, b, c, d, e, monuments 79-85
bis; *295 (cf. p. 523 supplement) are from Ostia and Portus. Vol. I
contains an introduction and conclusions. For a summary of the
material from Ostia cf. Vol. I, p. 265, n. 4. Cumont's conclusions,
without the notes, have been published separately; English translation
by T. J. McCormack: *The Mysteries of Mithra,* Chicago, 1903. In the
following discussion, references are to the larger work if no title is
given.

bly the oldest *Mithreum* in Ostia.[9] Its proximity to the temple of Magna Mater led Visconti to the conclusion that it was not a *Mithreum,* but was a shrine of the Phrygian gods which was used for initiations.[10] His view was not disputed until Cumont showed that the sanctuary was a *Mithreum.* The figures of the mosaic pavement of the central part of the shrine,[11] representing an old man with spade and scythe, a raven, a cock, a scorpion, a serpent, and a bull's head, Visconti tried to connect with Cybele and Attis. Cumont has shown, however, that the old man is probably Silvanus, who seems to have been identified with *Drvâspa* in the Mithraic religion,[12] and that the other figures of the mosaic are all well known in the cult of the Persian god. A beautiful head with a Phrygian cap found here, and now in the Lateran Museum, was thought by Visconti to represent Attis.[13] Cumont recognized in it a head of Mithras, probably from the group which stood at the end of the temple. The style of the head seems to date it in the time of Hadrian. A head of Sol, now in the Lateran, was also discovered in the *Mithreum.*

[9] Cumont, Mon. 295, pp. 414 ff., cf. p. 523. This shrine is listed by Cumont among *Monuments douteux,* although he seems not to doubt that it is a *Mithreum.* A plan of the temple is given by Cumont, II. Fig. 346; De Marchi, *Il Culto privato di Roma antica,* II. Tav. IV; Paschetto, *op. cit.* Fig. 109 (all after *Mon. dell'Inst.* VIII, Tav. LX.)

[10] *Ann. dell'Inst.* 1868, pp. 402 ff. Visconti called the temple a *sacrario metroaco* and believed that it was used for initiations into the cult of the Phrygian gods. He came to this conclusion the more readily because he believed that Mithras was worshiped in temples like those of other gods, as well as in the underground sanctuaries which were, he thought, for initiates only. De Marchi, *op. cit.* II. p. 153, does not seem to know Cumont's discussion of this shrine. Paschetto speaks of the shrine as a *Mithreum, op. cit.* p. 169, but on p. 375 he expresses doubt as to whether it is or not.

[11] Reproduced *Mon. dell'Inst. l. c.;* Cumont II. Fig. 347; De Marchi, *op. cit.* Tav. V; *Paschetto, op. cit.* Fig. 110.

[12] See discussion of Silvanus.

[13] *Mon. dell'Inst. l. c.,* Cumont, II. Figs. 348 and 490. Cf. also Benndorf and Schoene, *op. cit.* no. 547; Helbig, *Führer,* I. no. 717.

Cumont believes that the proximity of this *Mithreum* to the *Metroum* indicates a close connection between the cults of Magna Mater and Mithras at Ostia. Indeed he thinks that the south wall of the *Mithreum* may be a continuation of the north wall of the *Metroum,* and that the two buildings were probably constructed at the same time. Further evidence for the relationship of the two cults he finds in the inscription of a priest, apparently of Mithras, discovered in the *schola* of the *dendrophori* adjoining the *Metroum:* 70. . . . d. d. M. Cerellio Hieronymo patri et sacerdoti suo, eosque antistes s. s. deo libens dicavit. With regard to other inscriptions found in the *schola,* Cumont adds: " les divinités dont les noms sont mentionnés sur d'autres pierres (Virtus, Mars, Silvanus, Terra Mater) étaient toutes honorées dans la religion mithriaque, tandis que toutes sauf la dernière, paraissent étrangères aux mystères des dieux phrygiens. . . . Deux des inscriptions des dendrophores sont datées des années 142 et 143 ap. J. C. La consécration du mithréum, dont la présence permet seule de comprendre ces dédicaces, est donc antérieure au milieu du IIe siècle, ce qui concorde bien avec l'époque assignée par M. Visconti à la tête du prétendu Attis." [14]

Although there was undoubtedly a connection between the cults of Magna Mater and Mithras,[15] the evidence does not

[14] Cumont, II. p. 418. The inscriptions recording gifts of statues to the *dendrophori* (53, 69, 33, 70) are listed by Cumont among doubtful inscriptions. Cf. p. 475, nos. 560a, b, c, d, e. The occurrence of the title *mater* in 69 suggests to Cumont that there may have been at Ostia, as perhaps at Cologne, mysteries for women related to the mysteries of Mithras from which women seem to have been excluded. Cf. Cumont's note, II. p. 476, on inscr. 574b. Cumont does not mention 37, which records the gift of a statue of Attis to the *cannophori* by two people bearing the titles *pater* and *mater.* There seems to be no doubt that these titles were used in the cult of Magna Mater at Ostia, cf. discussion of Magna Mater. Wissowa, *Religion und Kultus,*[2] p. 369, n. 2, confuses the facts and states that the inscriptions bearing the dates 142 and 143 were found in the *Mithreum.*

[15] Cf. Cumont, *Mysteries,* pp. 86 f., pp. 179 f.

justify Cumont's conclusion that the two cults were particularly closely related at Ostia. The proximity of the two temples proves nothing, for another *Mithreum* of Ostia was situated directly behind four small temples with which it seems to have no connection. It is by no means certain that the two temples were built at the same time. Furthermore, the occurrence of the title *pater* among the worshipers of Magna Mater at Ostia suggests the possibility that the *pater et sacerdos* whose inscription was found in the *schola* may have been a priest of Magna Mater.[16] But even if the inscription is Mithraic—and the double title so often found in the cult of Mithras is in favor of this view—it may not have been placed in the *schola* originally. We have seen that some of the other inscriptions found there probably came from places near by. Moreover, there is no reason to believe that the dedication of statues of Virtus, Mars, and Silvanus to the *dendrophori* indicates a connection with the Persian god. We know that the *dendrophori* had special reason for honoring Silvanus.[17] Mars and Virtus, though they seem to have been identified with gods of the Persian Pantheon,[18] are each mentioned only once in Mithraic inscriptions, if we may trust Cumont's indices. The epigraphical evidence for dating the *Mithreum* before 142 is then far from convincing, though the style of the head of Mithras and the character of the remains favor the date Cumont proposes.

In excavations near the Torre Bovacciana in 1860-1861 a *Mithreum* was discovered in the ruins of a building which is generally—without good reason—called the Palazzo Imperiale.[19] In this building are extensive ruins of baths which have sometimes been thought to be the baths of Antoninus Pius, known to have been restored by the second P.

---

[16] See discussion of Magna Mater.

[17] See discussion of Silvanus.

[18] Cf. Cumont, I. pp. 143, 151.

[19] Cumont, Mon. 83, Inscr. 131-133. Visconti, *Ann. dell'Inst.* 1864, pp. 147 ff. Tav. d. Agg. K.

Lucilius Gamala.[20]   The date of a Mithraic inscription of
the year 162 found here would be in accord with the identification of the baths.   A niche of the pronaos of the temple
was adorned with a mosaic representation of Silvanus,[21]
which is now in the Lateran Museum.   In the black and
white mosaic pavement of the central portion of the interior
is written twice the inscription (56): Soli invict. Mit. d. d.
L. Agrius Calendio.   At the end of the sanctuary was an
altar with the inscription (57): C. Caelius Hermaeros
antistes huius loci fecit sua pec.   On each side of the central
portion of the *Mithreum* there were bases which supported
statues of the Mithraic torchbearers or *dadophori*.[22]   Similar *dadophori* are represented in relief on the bases, on each
of which occurs the inscription (58, 59): C. Caelius Erme-
ros antistes huius loci fecit sua pec.   On the left side of
one of these bases is the consular date 162 A. D.   Marble
fragments of a head with a Phrygian cap and of a right
hand holding a knife found here belonged to the group of
Mithras Tauroctonos which stood originally at the end of the
shrine.[23]

One of the richest *Mithrea* of Ostia was the one discovered
by the English painter Robert Fagan in 1797.[24]   Its exact
location is not known, but it seems to have been near Torre
Bovacciana.   We are told that it was entered through a
long narrow corridor, and that its form was in imitation of
a natural grotto.   At the entrance was found a group representing Mithras Tauroctonos which is now in the Galleria

[20] *CIL.* XIV 376.   For plan of the *Mithreum* cf. *Mysteries*, Fig. 16;
Mél. 1911, Pl. V; Paschetto, *op. cit.* Fig. 119.

[21] See discussion of Silvanus.

[22] Cumont, II. Fig. 72, 74; *Mysteries*, Fig. 18.

[23] Visconti, *l. c.*, p. 159.   Another statue of a *dadophoros*, now in the
Lateran, seems also to have been found here.   Cf. Paschetto, *op. cit.*
p. 392, n. 3; Benndorf and Schoene, *op. cit.* n. 586.

[24] Cumont, Mon. 79-81, Inscr. 137-139; Visconti, *Ann. dell'Inst.* 1864,
p. 151; Zoega, *Abhandlungen*, Taf. V. n. 15, p. 146.

Lapidaria of the Vatican.[25]   On the base of this relief is the
inscription (64) : Sig. indeprehensivilis dei L. Sextius Karus
et G. Valerius Heracles sacerdos s. p. p.   Within the shrine
was found a white marble statue of the Mithraic Kronos,
which is today at the entrance of the Vatican Library.[26]
The figure, which has a lion's head and four wings on which
are represented the signs of the seasons, is encircled six
times by a serpent.   On a projection of the base is the inscription (65) : C. Valerius Heracles pat. et C. Valerii
Vitalis et Nicomes sacerdotes s. p. c. p. s. r. d. d. idi. Aug.
imp. Com. VI et Septimiano cos (190 a. d.).   A bas-relief
representing a similar figure of a Mithraic Kronos was also
found here.[27]   From this *Mithreum* probably came also the
inscription (66) : C. Valerius Heracles pat[e]r e[t] an-
[tis]tes dei iu[b]enis inconrupti So[l]is invicti Mithra[e
c]ryptam palati concessa[m] sibi a M. Aurelio. . . .[28]
   A fragmentary bas-relief with Mithraic representations

[25] Cumont, ii. Fig. 67; Amelung, *Sc. des Vat. Mus.* i. p. 275, Gall.
Lapid. 144b, Taf. 30.
   [26] Cumont, ii. Fig. 68, cf. Vol. i, pp. 92-93; *Mysteries*, Fig. 20; Paschetto, *op. cit.* Fig. 34.
   [27] Cumont, ii. Fig. 69; Paschetto, *op. cit.* Fig. 114.
   [28] De Rossi wished to restore a M. Aurelio [*Commodo Antonino Aug.*]
but Dessau's view that this M. Aurelius was perhaps a freedman or
procurator of the emperor is much more probable.   Carcopino, *Mél.* 1911,
p. 219, notes that *palatium* would hardly be used of a private house,
and that if this M. Aurelius was a *procurator*, the building of which
the *Mithreum* was a part probably belonged to the emperor.   He believes
the *Mithreum* to be identical with the one discovered in 1860-1861 in
the so-called Palazzo imperiale—" malgré l'apparente contradiction chro-
nologique entre *CIL.* xiv 58-59 et *CIL.* xiv 65." He notes that the
latter *Mithreum* did not contain a Mithraic bas-relief.   As stated above,
however, fragments of such a bas-relief were found there.   Cumont has
also suggested that the *Mithreum* discovered by Fagan may be identical
with one mentioned by Visconti, *Ann. dell'Inst.* 1868, p. 412, which
could be seen " non molto lungi dai ruderi del teatro lungo una via
fatta tracciare per recarsi dalla prima piazza dell'antica città verso
il cosidetto tempio di Giove." Cf. Cumont, ii. p. 418, Mon. *295 bis.
This *Mithreum* is, however, connected by Paschetto (*op. cit.* p. 387)
with the shrine found in 1802.

on it was also discovered by Fagan apparently at Ostia, and is now in the Museo Chiaramonti of the Vatican.[29]

A relief of *pavonazzetto* representing Mithras Tauroctonos, now in the Galleria Lapidaria of the Vatican, was found at Ostia in the excavations of Pope Pius VII in 1802.[30] The circumstances of its discovery are not known, but it is probable that it was originally built into the wall at the end of a *Mithreum*. Above it was the inscription (60): A. Decimius A. f. Pal. Decimianus s. p. restituit, and below it (61): A. Decimius A. fil. Pal. Decimianus aedem cum suo pronao ipsumque deum solem Mithra et marmoribus et omni cultu sua p. restituit. At the same time were found: 62. L. Tullius Agatho deo invicto Soli Mithrae aram d. d. eanque dedicavit ob honore dei M. Aemilio Epaphrodito patre, and 63. M. Aemilio Epaphrodito patre et sacerdote.

Cumont has suggested that this *Mithreum* may be identical with the one discovered in a private house behind the four small temples in 1885-1886.[31] The fact that neither sculpture nor inscriptions were found in the latter supports the suggestion. This *Mithreum* is of great interest because of the mosaic representations which cover the central section and the *podia*. On the ends of the *podia* are the two *dadophori,* on the sides the six planets, and on top the twelve signs of the zodiac. In the central pavement are represented a sacrificial knife and seven half circles which indicate the seven celestial spheres. " A Ostie, sept demi-cercles,

---

[29] Cumont, II. Mon. 85, Fig. 78; Museo Chiaramonti, no. 569; cf. Amelung, *op. cit.* I, p. 692. Taf. 74. According to Amelung, a fragment in the Cortile del Belvedere n. 105 belongs with this one. Cf. also Zoega, *Abhandlungen*, p. 150, n. 25, pp. 176 f., who states that the relief was found at Quadraro.

[30] Cumont, II. Mon. 82, inscr. 134-136. Paschetto, *op. cit.* Fig. 115. Amelung, *op. cit.* Vol. I. p. 274, Taf. 30.

[31] Cumont, II. Mon. 84. Fig. 77; Lanciani, *NS.* 1886, pp. 162 ff.; Schierenberg, *Jahrbücher des Vereins f. Alt. Fr. im Rh.* 84, pp. 249 ff.; Cumont, *Notes sur un temple mithriaque découvert à Ostie*, Gand, 1891; Paschetto, *op. cit.* pp. 394 ff. Figs. 120, 121.

dessinés dans le pavement du choeur, marquaient sans doute les stations où le prêtre s'arrêtait pour invoquer les planètes, figurées sur la paroi des bancs." [32]

A shrine which is of the usual type of *Mithreum* was uncovered in 1908 on the road which leads from the Via dei Sepolcri to the baths.[33] Here were found inscriptions to Jupiter Sabazis [34] and Numen Caelestis,[35] but no Mithraic inscriptions or sculptures. Vaglieri, believing that other Oriental cults may have had shrines similar to those of Mithras, suggests that this may be a *Sabazeum*. He points out that the cult of Mithras is known to have influenced that of Sabazis. But since there is no evidence that Sabazis was ever worshiped in a temple of this type, it seems more probable that the shrine is a *Mithreum*.

An obscure inscription found near the theatre seems to refer to a restoration of a *spelaeum* or temple of Mithras. Cf. *NS*. 1910, pp. 186 f. Ma. Victori patri Aur. Cresces. Aug. lib. fratres ex speleo dilapso in meliori restauravit.[36] Two other inscriptions found recently, both fragmentary, may be dedications to Mithras.[37] One of them bears the consular date 107 A. D.

An inscription on an epistyle found at Ostia records the

---

[32] Cumont, I. p. 63.

[33] Vaglieri, *Comptes rendus des Séances de l'Académie des Inscriptions et Belles-Lettres*, 1909, pp. 184-191.

[34] *EE*. IX 439.

[35] *Ibid.* 436. Vaglieri's suggestion, *l. c.* p. 191, that the Numen Caeleste (?) may be Mithras cannot be supported. The epithet *caelestis* seems never to have been applied to Mithras. See p. 93.

[36] Vaglieri can hardly be correct in his suggestion that this may refer to the presentation of a statue of Mars to the *fratres*, for in that case the inscription would have been worded differently. Mars was identified with a Persian god. Cf. Cumont, I. pp. 143 f.

[37] *EE*. IX 441, 463. For another fragment of the second inscription see *NS*. 1911, p. 283. Cf. also *EE*. IX 444 .... Guntas fecerunt de sua pecuni[a. Vaglieri notes that the name Guntas is found in a Mithraic inscription of Rome.

dedication of a statue of Ahriman, the Mithraic evil spirit.[38]
Cf. *EE*. IX 433; L]olliano Callinico patre [P]etronius
Felix Marsus Signum Arimanium do. de. d.

Although no *Mithreum* has been discovered at Portus,
inscriptions found there indicate the existence of at least one
shrine.[39] A bronze tablet bears an inscription of a priest
of Mithras: 403. Sex. Pompeio Sex. fil. Maximo sacerdoti
Solis invicti Mi. patri patrum qq. corp. treiect. togatensium,
sacerdotes Solis invicti Mi. ob amorem et merita eius. Sem-
per habet. Above is represented a bust of Sol, on the right
a *patera,* on the left a sacrificial knife. A marble vase
found in the excavations of the Prince Torlonia bears the
inscription (55): Invicto deo S[oli]. A head of Sol and
a Mithraic *dadophoros* are represented on the vase. 286
gives an Album sacrato[rum] or list of members of a religious organization which is proved to be Mithraic by the
titles *pater* and *leo* found in it.

OTHER SOLAR DIVINITIES

Invictus Deus Sol. A fragmentary dedication was discovered in the Via del teatro: *EE*. IX 440. [invicto] deo Soli
[omnip]otenti ... o. caelesti n[u]m[ini p]raesenti Fo[r]-
tu[na]e Laribus Tut[ela]eque [sa]c [Venera]ndus.

Sol and Luna. On a tile which was built into a wall at
Portus is the inscription (4089.7): Ex oficin. L. Aemili
Iuliani Solis et Lunae sacerd. Since there is no other evi-
dence for a temple of Sol and Luna at Portus or at Ostia,
Iulianus may have been priest in some other place.[1]

[38] On Ahriman cf. Cumont, I. p. 139.
[39] *Cumont*, II. Mon. *85 bis, Inscr. 140-142.
[1] In 404, which is so fragmentary that it is unintelligible, are the
words *in Solis* n(umero).

SABAZIS

In a small shrine which was probably a *Mithreum* was discovered the inscription *EE*. IX 439: L. Aemiliu[s. . .]eusc ex imperio Iovis Sabazi votum fecit.

CAELESTIS

In the same shrine where an inscription to Sabazis was found,[1] the following dedication came to light: *EE*. IX 436. Numini c[ae]lesti P. Clodius [Fl]avius Venera[n]dus [2] VI vir [A]ug. somno monitus fecit. There seems to be no reason to doubt that this *numen Caelestis* [3] is the Dea Cae- lestis of Carthage, whose cult was fairly widespread. Vaglieri's suggestion that it refers to the Lydian Anaitis lacks support.[4] Two other cases of *numen Caelestis* certainly refer to the Carthaginian goddess.[5]

[1] See p. 91.

[2] Possibly the same man who set up *EE*. IX 440, in which the epithet *Caelesti* is used of some god.

[3] Vaglieri, *Comptes rendus*, 1909, p. 190, is probably wrong in taking *Caelestis* as an adjective here, and reading *numen caeleste* for the nominative form. *Caelestis* seems to be in apposition to *numen*.

[4] He would refer to Anaitis also the familiar inscription of the Capitoline, *NS*. 1892, p. 407. Cf. Frère, *Sur le culte de Caelestis*, *Rev. Arch*. x. 1907, p. 23.

[5] *CIL*. VIII 8239; III 992, cf. 993.

CONCLUSION

The various points established by this study have been embodied in the discussions of the individual cults. It remains by way of conclusion to indicate the cults of the colony which were honored with temples and shrines, and to point to the circumstances which produced the peculiar religious aspect of the colony.

The temples known to have existed at Ostia and Portus are those of Vulcan, the Capitoline Triad, Castor and Pollux, Liber Pater, Venus, Fortuna, Ceres, Spes, the Genius of the Colony, Roma and Augustus, Magna Mater, Isis, and Sarapis. There were also shrines of Pater Tiberinus, of the emperors Vespasian, Titus, Hadrian, Marcus Aurelius, and Septimius Severus,[1] and numerous shrines of Mithras. Of the temples, that of Sarapis and, probably, that of Liber Pater were at Portus; all the others seem to have been at Ostia. Certainly one shrine of Mithras was in Portus.

The cult of Vulcan, of the Capitoline Triad, and of Castor and Pollux seem to have been established early in the history of Ostia. Vulcan was probably worshiped in this region even before the foundation of the colony and must have remained for a long time the chief god of the city. Evidence for his preëminence is found in the fact that the *pontifex* of Ostia was called *pontifex Volcani et aedium sacrarum.* The *Capitolium,* where the great Etruscan Triad of the Capitoline Hill in Rome was worshiped, existed as early as the year 199 B. C. The fact that Ostia was a citizen colony probably accounts for the establishment of this cult, which was perhaps under the direction of the state. The cult of Castor and Pollux at Ostia—the only place where

---

[1] There was also a shrine of several emperors in the barracks of the *vigiles.*

the Dioskuri are known to have been worshiped as gods of the sea—was also a state cult, established perhaps as early as the third century B. C. when Ostia first became a harbor of importance. An annual festival in honor of Castor and Pollux was celebrated by the Roman people at Ostia.

There is little evidence to show when other temples were established. The temple of Roma and Augustus was built during the lifetime of Augustus. The shrines of the individual emperors must have been built shortly after the death of each emperor. If Carcopino's very doubtful dating of *CIL.* xiv 375 be accepted, temples of Venus, Fortuna, Ceres, and Spes were built during the first years of the Empire. For the other cults there is no evidence that can be dated earlier than the second century after Christ.

During the second and third centuries of our era—the period from which most of our evidence for the religion of Ostia dates—the Orient was exerting a strong influence on the religious life of the Romans.[2] At Ostia this influence is especially strong. It is seen in the early establishment and great prominence of the cult of the emperors which had its origin in the East, as well as in the strength of the purely Eastern worships. The most important of these gods at Ostia were Magna Mater, Isis, and Mithras. The monuments of the cult of Magna Mater there are second only to those of Rome in importance. Inscriptions give evidence for more devotees of Isis and the other Egyptian gods at Ostia than at any other place. The earliest datable *Mithreum* is there, and more *Mithrea* have been found there than anywhere else except at Rome.

The special importance of Eastern cults at Ostia at this time is not surprising in view of the fact that the city was then perhaps the world's greatest port.[3] Thither came mer-

---

[2] See Carter, *The Religious Life of Ancient Rome*, chap. 3.

[3] Cf. Florus i. 1, 4. Ancus Marcius – – – Ostiamque in ipso maris fluminisque confinio coloniam posuit, iam tum videlicet praesagiens animo futurum *ut totius mundi opes et commeatus illo velut maritimo urbis hospitio reciperentur.*

chants and mariners from the whole Mediterranean world. One would naturally expect to find in the port traces of the religious belief of these strangers, especially of those who came from the East.   Both Oriental merchants and Romans who traded in the East were apparently instrumental in spreading the picturesque religions of the East.   Thus the Egyptians who manned the grain fleet from Alexandria established at Portus a splendid *Sarapeum* modelled after the great temple at Alexandria.   Here too traders from Gaza seem to have worshiped their native god Marnas, whose cult is not known elsewhere outside of the East.

But the presence of merchants and sailors by no means adequately explains the relative importance of the religions of the port.   The Syrians, who formed the most important class of foreign merchants,[4] had very few shrines at Ostia. In fact Ostia was so near Rome that many of the passing foreigners apparently preferred to perform their devotions in the capital city[5] where there were splendid temples of their native gods.   This is probably the reason that at Ostia there are far fewer inscriptions of Syrian and Phoenician gods than at Puteoli, which was much farther from Rome. Furthermore the cults of Magna Mater and Mithras which flourished so vigorously at the port were not fostered preëminently by seafaring people, nor is it possible that they were introduced in the colony directly from the East. In fact Magna Mater had long been worshiped at Rome, and Mithras, too, if we may rely on inscriptional evidence, was worshiped at Rome before he was known at Ostia.   It would seem then that the relatively great importance of the Oriental cults at Ostia, as compared with other Italian municipalities, is to be explained by the nature of the

[4] Cf. Pârvan, *Die Nationalität der Kaufleute im römischen Kaiserreiche*, pp. 110 ff.; Blümner, *Römische Privataltertümer*, p. 633.
[5] There is definite evidence that this was the case with the Tyrians. Cf. *IG.* xiv 830.

population of the city rather than by the presence of passing strangers.

Now the special conditions and the time of Ostia's growth best explain the nature of its population. During the Republic when the native cults were still respected, the colony was still relatively small, and its inhabitants were probably not wealthy enough to build magnificent temples. When, owing to the harbor improvements of Claudius and Trajan, the city began to grow, the native Roman gods had lost much of their hold upon the people. This loss was due in part to the skepticism which had spread throughout Italy, but also to the fact that the native stock of Italy, which might have supported the purely Roman cults, had dwindled greatly. The thousands who came to find employment at the docks, warehouses, and shops of the growing port must have been very largely ex-slaves and descendants of slaves of Oriental stock. This class of people had practically gained control of Rome's retail business even before our era, and were now rivalling the Oriental merchants in Italy's foreign trade.[6] Many of these people became members of the various collegia at Ostia, and often as *dendrophori* or *Augustales* obtained a position of importance in the community.

The cults of Magna Mater and of Mithras, and, to a lesser extent, that of Isis were then chiefly supported at Ostia, as was regularly the case elsewhere, by freedmen or descendants of freedmen of Eastern origin. Even though many of them may have abandoned their native religions during their life as slaves, they were by nature more inclined to the emotional cults of the East than to the more formal Roman worships. The great importance of these cults at Ostia is then to be attributed to the large proportion of such classes among the inhabitants of the colony.

---

[6] Cf. Pârvan, *op. cit.* p. 39; Kühn, *De opificum Romanorum condicione privata*. Dissertation, Halle, 1910; Friedländer, *Sittengeschichte Roms*, I.⁸ p. 302.

These new religions did not entirely drive out the old.[7] The chief priest of the colony still continued to be called pontifex of Vulcan, and he had jurisdiction even over the temples of the foreign gods. Throughout the second century Roman knights and *decuriones* continued to hold the old priestly titles of *praetor* and *aedilis sacris Volcani faciundis*. *sodalis Arulensis, sacerdos geni coloniae, flamen,* and apparently were not numbered among the priests of the Oriental gods. Furthermore none of these priesthoods seem to have been held by priests of the Eastern gods. But as the worshipers of these cults grew in position and in wealth, they also lent dignity to the religions which they fostered. Hence during the later empire among the priests of Isis at Ostia was a man of senatorial rank. Thus the cults of the East which had long made a strong appeal to the masses became at last firmly established.

[7] It is not improbable that the strength of the Eastern cults at Ostia reduced the number of votaries of Vulcan. Certainly that god retained nothing of the hold on the inhabitants that Fortuna Primigeneia did at Praeneste or Hercules Invictus at Tibur.

BOOKS
OF
SIMILAR INTEREST

THE ROMAN WORLD

IMPERIAL ROME. *Martin P. Nilsson.*

A completely fresh outlook on Roman history, this book features thorough, yet brief, biographies of all the Roman emperors in the first part. The second part describes the provinces of the empire, their individual circumstances and their histories, as well as a series of essays on politics, finances, religion, customs, etc. Written by the masterful hand of a great scholar, it is one of the most comprehensive works available on the many facets of the life, people, and customs of the Roman Empire. A useful and reliable handbook for both the student of history and the numismatist.

ISBN 0-89005-054-6. 376 pp. + 24 pl. $15

ROMAN PROVINCIAL ADMINISTRATION. *W. T. Arnold.*

A sobering account of the mishandling of the Roman Empire's finances as we watch Roman economic history being paralleled in our own times. Each month Arnold's work takes on dimensions of increasing importance. Particular attention is given to the coinage laws, inflation, price stabilization edicts and their effects on the Roman economy. The politics, administration, causes and effects of economic and other laws are carefully scrutinized to give us insights valuable today. Of special interest to the student of Roman history, the collector of Roman coins, students of economics, and those who wonder where our own economy may be headed.

ISBN 0-89005-027-9. 298 pp. $15

THE PROVINCES OF THE ROMAN EMPIRE.
Theodor Mommsen.

This is a reprint of the 1909 edition of the *complete work,* authorized and translated into English under Mommsen's supervision. One of the greatest ancient historians at his best! No other work on the subject offers such a careful analysis of historical, economic, cultural and religious aspects of the Roman provinces. A well organized presentation which skillfully blends a multitude of diverse historical facts into a logical panorama of the Roman provinces and their place in ancient history.

Vol. I, ISBN 0-89005-051-1.
Vol. II, ISBN 0-89005-152-X. 756 pp. 2 vols. $30

LATIN EPIGRAPHY. *J. E. Sandys.*

The standard introductory treatise on Latin inscriptions, their interpretation, and value as authentic sources of history. Essential to the study and understanding of Latin inscriptions, this is a leading source book in the field and contains an extensive listing of abbreviations and a complete record of cursus honorum of every emperor.
ISBN 0-89005-062-7. 96 pp. $10

TRADE ROUTES AND COMMERCE OF THE ROMAN EMPIRE. *M. P. Charlesworth.*

The fascinating story of Imperial Rome's struggle to become economic master of its rapidly acquired overseas empire and balance its foreign trade. A valuable and authoritative work for information on the commercial life of the Roman Empire, voyage time from place to place, and both wise and foolish trade policies of the Romans. Many interesting parallels to the trade and economic policies of major world powers in our own times.
ISBN 0-89005-063-5. 320 pp. $10

THE ELDER PLINY'S CHAPTERS ON THE HISTORY OF ART. Translated by *K. Jex-Blake* and *E. Sellers.*

As delightful and useful today as it was to Roman tourists who took it along while exploring their empire nearly 2,000 years ago. Time has proven Pliny's work to be the keystone reference for the study of ancient Greek Sculpture. Pliny's original Latin text is given with a facing English translation together with commentaries on what ancient sculptures have been identified in the later times on the basis of his descriptions. Updated with a new *Introduction* and *Select Bibliography* (1896-1974) by R. V. Schoder, S.J., of Loyola University. Since many of the sculptures Pliny describes also appear on ancient coins, this work addresses itself to the numismatist as well as the art historian and student of the classics.
ISBN 0-89005-055-4. 252 pp. $12.50

OUTLINE HISTORY OF GREEK RELIGION. *L. R. Farnell.*

This excellent handbook explains in easy terms the basic trends of the ancient Greek religion, its rites, influence on society and culture as well as the origins of their gods and myths. Essential for understanding the Greeks and their mythology. An ideal text for introductory courses on Greek mythology.
ISBN 0-89005-025-2. 160 pp. $7.50

IMPERIAL ROMAN COIN TYPES AND INSCRIPTIONS.
Comm. Gnecchi, H. Cohen, G. Elmer, et al.

A compendium and translation of works by noted experts on Roman coins. A source book for the beginning or advanced collector *and* the perfect reference for the non-numismatist seeking vital information found on Roman coins. Georg Elmer's tables listing all coins struck by each emperor, regnal dates, etc. appear for the first time in English. Gnecchi's *Coin Types of Imperial Rome* and H. Cohen's listings of reverse coin inscriptions have great value to historians, archaeologists and numismatists alike. The text is greatly enhanced by the plates of British Museum specimens used by Harold Mattingly. The most complete reference work on Imperial Roman coins available anywhere.

    ISBN 0-89005-047-3. 226 pp. + 44 pl. + tables   *$10*

THE ROMANS ON THE RIVIERA AND THE RHONE.
W. H. Hall.

Reprint of the extremely rare edition of 1898 (London). There is no other book in the English Language which describes more vividly or more accurately the history of the long struggle of the Roman Republic for the conquest of the part of Southern Gaul which later became the "Provincia" and still later the "Gallia Narbonensis." Hall has a first-hand knowledge of the topography of the French Riviera and its coastline as well as a complete knowledge of the Roman ruins, monuments and inscriptions. He gives the best possible history of the area during the Roman period and describes minutely the process of its Romanization.

    ISBN 0-89005-022-8. 208 pp. + 16 pl. + maps   *$10*

MITHRAIC ART. A Search for Unknown and Unidentified Monuments. *Al. N. Oikonomides.*

Believing that many monuments of Mithraic art in museums of the old and new world still remain unidentified and incompletely interpreted as such, the author has collected a number of studies in this volume devoted to typical cases. Special sections examine the birth of the Mithraic family, the cult of Mithra in Marseilles, Mithra in Roman Athens, Mithra on the royal coinage of Pontus and other areas of the Mithraic cult and its artistic legacy.

    ISBN 0-89005-081-3, 96 pp. *$7.50*

CULTS AND CREEDS IN GRAECO-ROMAN EGYPT.
H. Idris Bell.

Valuable information from ancient papyri on the previously confused history of the religions and cults of Graeco-Roman Egypt. Special sections on the pagan amalgam. Jews in Egypt and the rise of Christianisty.

LC 75-21018. ISBN 0-89005-088-0. 128 pp. $10.00
Student edition $6.00

THE RELIGION OF GREECE. *Th. Zielinski.*
Covers the spectrum of Greek deities and their relationship to the deification of nature, consecration of work and the revelation of God in beauty and goodness. A special section treats the influence of Greek religion on modern society and thought.

LC 75-24017, ISBN 0-89005-090-2, 248 pp. $10.00
Student edition $6.00

CHRISTIAN EPIGRAPHY. *Orazio Marucchi.*
Translated by *J. Armine Willis.*

With its new, enlarged format, this is the best guide to the formulas used to interpret and date early Christian documents, symbols and abbreviations. Richly illustrated, Marucchi's work is the only available introductory handbook in English which examines the field of early Greek and Latin Christian inscriptions in depth.

ISBN 0-89005-070-8. 472 pp. + 30 pl. $15

HISTORIA REIPUBLICAE MASSILIENSIUM.
Henricus Ternaux.

Reprint of the extremely rare edition of 1826 (Goettingen). Written in scholarly Latin, this monograph remains one of the most important books on the history and antiquities of the ancient city of Massalia (Marseilles). Ternaux has collected from the ancient Greek and Latin sources almost everything mentioned about Massalia, Massaliot life and trade, colonization and local cults, mythology and history. Considered as an essential reference for the student of western Greek colonization, it is also an invaluable help to the student of Hellenization of the southern coast of Gallia and northern Spain. A limited edition, beautifully printed and bound.

ISBN 0-89005-038-4. 128 pp. $10

ARES PUBLISHERS Inc.

612 N. MICHIGAN AVE.   Suite 216
CHICAGO, ILLINOIS 60611   (312) 642-7850